PR/

One of the most direct, honest, and God-centered books you will read this year. Chara knows who she is. Firm in her identity, she will guide you through the exchange of loneliness and insecurity for the acceptance and authentic freedom you have longed for. It took guts to write these chapters. It will take guts for you to read it so you can toss out the guilt and start living in God's grace. Take this leap. Go all in. You are going to love the outcome.

—Jeremiah & Teresa Yancy,
Pursuing Jesus Ministries

Waves of impartation flooded over me as I read *Loved*. I found fresh faith to believe as a child and shamelessly walk in my personal identity. God's voice became louder, and I began to intimately hear Him speak to me through dreams and His still small voice. You are invited to join Chara on her journey into the engulfing love of God and find Him championing the child He uniquely created you to be.

—Kevin Wells, MEd/ Editor/Pastor

Chara writes with a candid simplicity that draws the reader into her story. The child-like joy in her words is palpable, and the spiritual insights she shares from within her journey are both insightful and inspiring.

—Richard Jones, Fatherheart Ministries

Absolutely amazingly transformative and so much revelation. I can't even describe what God has been saying to me about my own heart and life. The words were alive, life-giving and breathing, surrounded by His love. It made me cry, but it was a cry of freedom.

—Rhonda Martens

Captivating! There is an inspiring call in this book to live more from your heart and from God's endless source of love. This book will soften your heart in fresh ways and lead you forward into a deeper freedom, rest and vulnerability.

—Jesse Lerch, pastor, Junction Church

Weeping, weeping, is what I am doing as I read this - not of sadness, but of release and joy! The words Father left me with were, "HE IS ENOUGH." These words are a gift and I will reread them many times.

—Connie Johnson

Wow! I was captivated and couldn't put the story down. Chara has such a beautiful way of drawing us into her life and into the heart of God. I especially loved how she shared her deepest thoughts and feelings, always enveloped by the love of Jesus, Father and Holy Spirit. It touched my heart deeply and I was moved to tears. It felt so good to read this and to feel the Father's Love come through her words and bring me comfort. Chara has a way of connecting her heart to His and yet it connects to mine as well. Thank you, Chara, for sharing your vulnerability and for giving us a glimpse into your life and your sweet relationship with the trinity. I have been deeply touched.

—Debbie Christiansen

Chara is passionate about intimacy with the Father and when you read her journey, the gift that she has for explaining this passion may touch you in surprising ways. Her vulnerability invites you to observe, and perhaps experience, how the power of love allows transformation to unfold.

—Linda Schmidt

This book is a gift to those who long to know what it's like to live each day deeply and tangibly connected to God, receiving healing and freedom in the process. Chara holds nothing back as she invites the reader into her story of personal struggle and tragedy. She courageously shares the intimate details of how God healed her heart as she depended on His loving presence in her life moment by moment, day by day. Through sharing the revelation and keys that transformed her life, Chara casts hope that healing through the experienced reality of God's love is also for you.

—Annalisa Coyle

Wow, I'm hooked! This is incredible, I looooong for this:

> *"I am discovering a secret to freedom, and that is surrendering to the love of God, knowing He is loving me right now. I am caught in the flow of His transforming love. And freedom is the most beautiful word I know because here I am learning a new perspective on life—as a child*

> *loved by my Father. He is bringing me into His heart where I find safety and belonging. Inviting Him into lonely and insecure places is transforming them into jewels called acceptance and confidence. It's a refreshing way to live."* —excerpt from *Loved.*

I love Chara's intimate time with God. Her writing inspires a desire in me to find God's presence right now. I have excitement as my relationship grows with our beloved Father. I also love the part about loneliness being an issue of not being connected to our own hearts. Because this is true for so many, I think it will resonate and start a healing process.

—Liz Venz, CEO, Jack Nadel International

Chara's testimony is so powerful, it exudes freedom on every page! Never before have I felt such permission to simply be myself.

—Catherine Taylor

loved.

LOVED.

A TRUE STORY OF FINDING SELF ACCEPTANCE AND REAL FREEDOM

CHARA PRESLEY

messenger
BOOKS

Disclaimer: *This is a memoir, and the events and conversations in this book have been set down to the best of the author's ability.*

ISBN: 978-1-953314-07-9

Library of Congress Control Number: 2020917375

Published by:

Messenger Books
1629 Brookhollow, Dr.
Lindale, TX 75771
www.messengerbooks.com

messenger BOOKS

CONTENTS

I dedicate this book to my children, Brett and Jenna, and to their children after them. You have taught me much about joy and freedom, and the wonder of who you are fascinates me. I bless you to be all of who God created you to be as your hearts rest deeply in His love.

I also dedicate this book to all of God's children around the world. May you experience the passionate and protective love of our Father and rest in His strong hands. He is a good Father.

ACKNOWLEDGMENTS

I thank Father for hearing the cry of my heart to be free from the prison of being choked in my personality, strangled by shame and insecurity, and hidden under a blanket of self-condemnation. Thank You, Jesus, for loving me, and making me one with You, a child of the Father, loved, seen, accepted and free. Thank You for leading me in this incredible journey into freedom. I am ecstatic about Your love which frees me to be all that You created me to be.

Thank you to Messenger Books for coming alongside and unlocking the book inside of me. Your inspiration and practical insight made this a delightful experience.

Thank you to my "Dream Team" for believing in me. Thank you to Annalisa for knowing that I had a story to tell when I had no clue and for your attention to detail. Thank you, Catherine, for your honesty in telling me what didn't sound right and for your insightful questions. Thank you, Linda, for your big picture view on the chapters which helped my vision.

Thank you to my family who read my chapters, and cried and laughed, shocked that I could write - me, too! I believed in myself because you believed in my writing. Thank you for your blessing, Mom and Dad, which brought light and revelation so that I could keep writing when I got stuck. You are incredible parents.

Thank you to my children, Brett, Karina, Jenna, & Michael, who put up with running my thoughts past you and for your honest feedback. You are awesome.

Thank you to my husband, Michael, who happily laughed at my dancing after a day of writing in the Spirit and who lets me completely be myself.

I love you all.

Chara

FOREWORD

With grit, softness, tears, and triumph, but most of all, vulnerability and courage, Chara magnificently captures the everyday challenges of life. She takes you on a journey through the daunting young adult years of seeking to find belonging and purpose in the world. Chara speaks openly of her personal challenges of being a woman, mom, and wife, and how she found strength, comfort, and guidance in her faith to respond positively in her struggles.

In this unfiltered, real-life adventure, Chara bares her soul about her loss and shares the pangs of grief that can be debilitating for so many. It is a tender description of the shattering aspects of loss and the reality of living suspended between life and death – a true account of trying to make sense of life when a part of you dies. Through its sensitivity, her story offers the perspective that in Him, our response to death can be filled with grace, wisdom, joy, and sweet surrender.

The tales of her raw experiences get you in the back of your throat and deep in your belly as you identify those moments and times in your own relationships that felt so intense and hopeless, where nothing you did worked and how the only way forward was to "fall on His grace." Only His life flowing through you becomes your dependable life map.

Through her story, Chara shares with us that total dependence on the Father's love is the everyday oxygen we need to thrive. My hope is that we step out of those things that complicate our faith and join Chara in letting go and freefalling into His healing love.

Captivating, honest, provocative and inviting, this book challenges you to unlearn everything you have been taught about self preservation. It shows you in a beautiful and delicate expression that the only way to live in freedom is to let go of what you know and embrace His design for you. Chara's story is an exquisite example of what divine alliance, surrender and joyful moment by moment living looks like. She is freefalling everyday – and so will I!

—Abby Silva, MACP
Registered Clinical Counsellor (RCC)

INTRODUCTION

My life in Christ is the story of my Father and what He has done. He is lovingly and patiently molding my heart into a home designed only for Him and me. This is for His glory and a work He delights in and is even passionate to do.

One by one, the issues of my heart have been brought to my awareness, usually in anguish, doubt, fear or pain. I didn't consider these things friends at the time, but from where I stand now, I am so grateful for the purposes they served. For unhappiness, in all of its forms, is the thing that brought me to my knees before God. Some issues took decades to resolve in me, and even now, I sense I may be breaking a new barrier out of unworthiness, or perhaps it is shame, by putting my story in writing. I don't need to know what He is doing because He is at work in me, and I'm doing my best to simply follow His lead.

If unhappiness is so helpful, then why is it that I am so desperate to avoid pain? Perhaps it is because we were designed to live in the Father's overflowing joy and a depth of His love that satisfies our hearts. This is our true north. We are magnetically attracted to things that fill our hearts. Once we discover something that does, we hang onto it, maybe at all costs, like we are addicted. For me, some of these heart-stirrers were traveling, "best" friends, falling in love, a romantic marriage, excellence in my career, and even close relationships with my sisters or friends. These things are all completely wonderful, but to what degree do I find fulfillment in them? How easily can I be hurt by them? If I can be hurt, angry, jealous, and so on by disappointments, then maybe I am not yet free from idolizing the value they give to me.

It's amazing to think that my Father is working in my heart to remove the things that will disappoint me and bring me pain. At least, the impact of disappointment is significantly less when I am not relying on them alone to fill my heart with acceptance, belonging, and love. When God is in His proper place as Father in my heart, He will never disappoint me, and even when trouble comes, I can trust Him to lead me through.

One thing I understand much more clearly is that I seem to depend on all kinds of things to make me happy, and, to varying degrees, I can miss out on having perfect peace, the overflowing joy, and glory in the presence of the Holy Spirit. Still, I have touched on His beauty and found miraculous discoveries in my ordinary life. Jesus really is enough. I have discovered that in Him we can face anything life throws at us and we can always trust Him to guide us safely through.

I remember when He first showed me He was real, or rather, when the truth finally landed inside of me. I said to Him: "I need You because I don't know how to survive disasters, like death, coming to me during my life. Well, He has taken me on a great journey that only looks beautiful in retrospect. I am amazed. He loosened things from my heart that were clinging on for dear life so that I can experience Him in their place. I love our home in my heart. I am safe here with Him.

This journey is about letting go and venturing into unknown territory towards true significance. At its core, it is about freedom to be who God originally created me to be. To me, this means I am one with my Father Who loves me, I am the beloved bride of Christ, and His Holy Spirit presence lives in me. Because He delights in me, I delight in myself.

Opening your heart and listening with the heart of a child, positions you to allow yourself to be found by Him. I would love to share my story with you in hopes that you might connect with what God is doing in your heart.

You belong in His family.
You are included in His heart.
He accepts you as you are.
You are safe in His love.

I invite you to travel with me through my story and intermingle it with your story.

Believe He has freedom for you, too.

ONE
FOUND

Here's what I've learned through it all: Don't give up; don't be impatient; be entwined as one with the Lord. Be brave and courageous, and never lose hope. Yes, keep on waiting—for he will never disappoint you!
—*Psalm* 27:14—

"Come out of hiding—You're safe here with me."[1]
—From "Out of Hiding"—

As a self-assured, confident young woman at the age of nineteen, listening to the explorations in Europe of a college friend, my heart awakened to a desire to explore. This was the mid-80s, before the internet, when the world was much larger and vastly unknown, certainly at least to me. I didn't even know how to imagine Europe—my mind just had a blank canvas. I cried into my pillow every night at the thought of entering an unknown land all alone, leaving the security of home and family and all I knew behind. Yet, the longing for adventure and a dream of wandering free as a gypsy compelled me to go. My heart was resolute, and fear would not hold me back.

Before cell phones and the invention of the Global Positioning System (GPS), I quickly discovered that my handrails were my travel book, *Let's Go Europe*, a budget of $10 a day, and connections made with beautiful people everywhere, especially travelers in youth hostels. For the first time in my life, the only agenda on my plate every day was to follow my heart. Every morning was a fresh new day that unfolded naturally. Whatever I wanted to do, I did. Unless, of course, it cost money. That was one thing I didn't have much of, yet I wasn't seeking tourist sights and activities. I thought the purpose of life was to have fun. My heart was happy to see the land, walk the streets, visit untold historical sights, and connect heart to heart with people from all over the world.

Thirty five years later, I am coming back to living in the moment, one day at a time, discovering joy in connecting with people and wondering at the beauty and mystery in the world. No wonder I found such joy in traveling! It wasn't that I had no responsibilities; it was that I was free of "should"— obligations, duties, and the weighing down of how I ought to act when it wasn't what my heart wanted to do. It's amazing how, without realizing it, we can wander so far from our hearts.

I couldn't have known what was hidden inside my heart at the young age of nineteen. I knew some kind of a weight pressed on me daily, making me feel self-conscious and insecure. In chatting with someone, either a guy or girl, I usually found my face going red without even knowing why. I tried my best to ignore it, but it was humiliating. I would imagine that people thought I was boring or I would criticize myself for saying the wrong thing. I often think of it as feeling 'less than.' However, this was my normal life, and I simply managed it the best I could by forgetting about it. My favorite strategy was telling myself that in three days, no one would remember, including myself. It didn't stop me from getting on a plane by myself to Europe with my nine-hundred dollars tucked safely in my travel pouch.

ALONE IN FRANKFURT

With my backpack strapped on my hips and a map in hand, I nervously stepped into a subway station for the very first time in Frankfurt, Germany. Whizzing underground, somehow I found the correct exit, which was something "strasse." I quickly was lost in the crowd of people swarming into the streets, amazed to have arrived in the city center. Everything was in German, and I felt so small, alone, and afraid, as well as lost. I had no idea which direction to go. Trying unsuccessfully to hold back tears, I tried to ask busy strangers for directions to the youth hostel. To my dismay, one after another, I was ignored. My eyes blurred as I tried to calm my mind and not become overwhelmed. I was surrounded by elegant looking shops and what seemed in my vulnerability to be unfriendly business people walking exceptionally fast. Having grown up in a village of 2,000 people and then moving to a town with a population of 10,000, downtown Frankfurt was a lonely place.

Eventually, a kind man paused long enough to understand my English, then pointed me in the right direction and continued on his way. Tears were still soaking my cheeks, but feeling somewhat encouraged, I walked until I found the quiet refuge of the youth hostel. Immediately, I relaxed and began a discovery into the whole new world of backpackers, a band of like-minded adventurers and a subculture all of its own. The women slept in a large room of bunks where we chatted about travel ideas. Before I knew it, I had found a companion, and together, we set off for the "Romantic Road" bus in the morning, walking through fairytale villages preserved from times gone past. My journey had launched with an unimaginable momentum.

Following the wind proved to be not only fun, but life giving in its spontaneity. However, every once in a while, I was stunned by people's negativity, naively shocked at their behavior towards me. One time, I was in Paris walking around with my backpack as usual, and I stopped at a kiosk to ask for directions.

> "Où est le Champs-Elysées?" I asked.
> "@#!!#!" a woman replied sharply.
> "Où est le Champs-Elysées?" I repeated.
> "@#^#@*!" she quipped, clearly irritated.
> "Excusez-moi, je ne comprends pas, où est le Champs-Elysées?" I timidly asked for the third time.
> "BLAH BLAH BLAH!!!" she exploded at the top of her lungs.

Shocked and frightened at her intensity, I stumbled away. But the beauty of these encounters was that I discovered I could leave their discouraging impact behind and continue on to a new day, a new city, and new connections. What freedom this was, even if I had to be on the run to keep it!

In spite of these stories, once I got going, most people were surprisingly generous and kind. I've slept in train stations, on boats, in compassionate strangers' houses, even tucked into the curve of a cold subway cement floor. Wherever I went, a momentum of peace and expectation of joy followed. This was life-changing for me; I was gaining a new perspective and broadening my world. But I realize now that my experience of freedom was only maintained with an illusion created by my continual need to move. Backpacking from place to place lightened my heart and grew confidence in me. These are things which helped me for a time, and they were good, but they were like crutches, serving only a temporary purpose.

I AM PROTECTED

There really is a union with God through all our lives. The Father was there with me on my backpacking journey, though I didn't yet know Him. He saved me from disaster many times. I was once surrounded by a group of Northern African men one night in a Parisian alley. My heart beat in terror. Not understanding their words, but feeling their intentions, I sputtered innocently in broken French, "I'm on my way to my room! I'm staying here! I'm from Canada!"—all the while knowing they didn't understand me. Suddenly, inexplicably, they broke the circle around me and walked away. Phew! I was so thankful.

I spent the winter living communally on a kibbutz in northern Israel. My job was to cook breakfast for the cotton workers in a field about ten minutes away. After making a breakfast of eggs, thick yogurt, full-fat labneh (cottage cheese), fruit, homemade bread, tomatoes, cucumber, and olives, I decided to naively hitchhike back to the kibbutz. A shiny, red semi truck immediately stopped, and an Arab driver beckoned me to jump in. I was wearing green Israeli army clothes that I picked up in the second-hand bin. I felt the driver's eyes on me like a magnet. Looking firmly ahead, I said, "Kibbutz Dan." I spent the entire ride pushing his hands away and continuing to stare unswervingly at the road. With relief, I jumped out at my destination only to find a car screeching to a halt right behind me.

"What do you think you are doing?!" shouted one of the cotton workers. "I saw you from my tractor and ran to catch the guy's license plate number and speed after his truck in case something happened to you. What's wrong with you— don't you know how dangerous that is?!" Suitably chastened, I smiled with relief that I was being looked after, even in my own poor judgment.

Afterwards, I remember sitting on a rock ledge on the kibbutz, feeling a connection with the peaceful orange sunset. I was struck with a new sensation of God's presence. I sat there wondering if it really was God. It felt free and light, and I loved the experience. I cannot explain why I did not respond in faith to Him at the time, but He certainly was patient and never abandoned me, in spite of my faithlessness.

STOLEN BACKPACK

Sometimes, a temporary disaster turns out to be a gift from heaven. I spent the night on a Spanish train before my birthday with a Canadian girl with whom I felt immediate camaraderie. We shared stories late into the night and dozed on each other's shoulders.

As it became light, I heard her rummaging in the rack above my head. I intuitively felt that I should open my eyes and see what was happening, but I refused because I wanted to sleep so I would feel rested on my birthday. I popped my eyes open to say goodbye to my new friend as she got off at her stop. Soon, I woke and noticed that my pack was missing from above my head. I asked the Spanish people, who didn't speak English, what had happened to my backpack. They motioned that my friend had taken two bags. Dread flooded my heart as I sat there, feeling naked and poor in my lone purple tracksuit with my passport and twenty dollars tucked safely inside my shirt.

I cried helplessly as I pulled out my passport to show them it was my birthday, since they didn't understand my English. They kindly shared with me delicious dark chocolate which they ate on fresh bread.

I will never forget that birthday and the lonely feeling of walking up the wide street in Barcelona, my tears joining the raindrops pouring onto my face. She was even from Vancouver, near my own home town, and the experience of broken trust left me shattered. It felt strange walking along with nothing at all except the clothes on my back and the shoes on my feet, twenty dollars, and my passport, all of which I was thankful for.

Years later, I was resting gratefully on my couch at home while my 1-year-old son was asleep. I felt that I should go check on him, but I was too tired to lift my head. Suddenly, I thought, "I've had this feeling before." I recognized that gut feeling from the Spanish train experience, and without hesitating, ran up the stairs to my toddler's room. My son's cookie monster bed sheet was wrapped tightly around his head, and he was gasping for air with a horrible grating sound, still asleep.

Quickly, I unraveled him, noticing the blue spots around his eyes from his exertion to breathe. In a moment, he rested peacefully, and I was ecstatic that my backpack had been stolen so that I could sense something was wrong and save my baby's life. I knew that it was God at work in me both times, and though I had failed to listen to Him in Spain, now I knew the importance of listening to His voice.

> ***We must live in the Holy Spirit and follow after him.***

—Galatians 5:25

FOUND

Being "found" by my Father is a theme I delight to rest in everyday. I believe He is attracted to every open heart, although there are so many ways in which my heart has run from Him, simply desiring happiness, peace, or fulfillment. But like the Good Shepherd who went looking for his lost sheep, He also found me.

My first beautiful experience with God was when I was 12 years old at a Christian camp curled up in my sleeping bag on my bunk bed. For two weeks, I had been marveling at the atmosphere of acceptance and belonging. On the last night, my faith in Jesus became clear, and I decided to invite Him into my heart. My camp counselor, a brown-haired teenage girl, led me in a simple, heartfelt prayer. To my surprise, all night long I felt protected inside of an invisible glass cover, much like Snow White. I felt so light, clean, and pure. I don't think I moved all night as I was in such awe. However, in the morning, it went away. We swept our cabins and went home. My camp experience soon became a distant memory. As time went on, I decided I couldn't accept some of the teachings in the Bible and wasn't sure if Christianity made sense.

Years later in university, my good friend, Debbie, invited me to attend church. Feeling the presence of God, I suddenly knew He was real and was excited to pray, "Father, forgive me for my sins and please come into my life." I was beyond excited. I lapped up the Scriptures, and for two months, my heart was hungry and open to Him. However, there was a battle between the Presence I was drawn to and the thought "what will people think of me?"

My heritage is Russian Doukhobor Orthodox, and I had only known my "Baba," which is what I called my Grandmother, to speak Russian my whole life. She was living with us, and when I came home one day from church, she was waiting at the kitchen counter. I had never communicated with her without my parents interpreting.

Miraculously, this one morning, she began telling me how much God loved me and how good it was that I knew God. She opened her Russian Bible, pointing to the page, and in tears, she opened her heart to me, saying, "Whenever I feel lonely, I read my Bible, and I'm not lonely anymore!" And her greatest heart cry was for me to "tell Mama God loves her!!" We were both crying at this point. This truly was a miraculous sign from God that He was real.

However, my heart was in a war. The insecurity I felt was an open door for shame and a fiery need to be accepted by others, even though no one had said a thing. Not long after, I gave in to my fears, in spite of a wonderful visit from my friend from college, who drove eleven hours to Nelson, British Columbia, to encourage me in my faith. Sadly, I was still afraid of what my family and everyone would think of me, and with relief, I shut the door to God.

It was like a wall had gone up. Yes, there was an emptiness, but once I decided to turn away, I felt the door close. I didn't really realize that I myself had put up a wall just to keep myself away from God. While it lasted, I enjoyed the stirring of my spirit, His occasional presence, and the drawing to know more, but more than that, out of my insecurity, I wanted to ensure I was accepted by my family, who had not yet met God.

In the months after I turned my back on God, I began wondering about Him. Every night as I drifted off to sleep, I would generally pray, "God, if You're real, show me." Little did I know what He had in store for me. At the age of twenty-nine, I was still praying for God to show me if He was real.

I was holding my first baby, Brett, in my arms for the first time in the hospital. Immediately, waves of love were crashing in my heart for him, and in that moment I knew that God was real. God hadn't answered most of my questions, but He had increased my faith. Beyond a doubt, I saw this love was from God. To me, evolution could not offer an explanation for this powerful love evolving from specks of dust. I knew now that there would be no more back and forth for me. I may not have known much, but in that moment, I knew that love was from God.

> ***So we have come to know and to believe the love that God has for us. God is love, and whoever abides in love abides in God, and God abides in him.***
>
> **—1 John 4:16**

Life as a Christian was thrilling. I was excited during my baby's nap time to read and discover what was in the Bible. I was like the train in the story, "The Little Engine that Could" that chugged up the steep mountain repeating to himself, "I think I can, I think I can, I think I can..." I was caught up in a relentless conquering of the Christian life, and I loved it. Although I didn't understand it at the time, Christ was in union with me. I had not yet learned much about surrender, letting go of control, and learning how to let Him lead me. Some things were automatically happening in me, like my taste for certain TV shows just went away. I would have been astounded if I had known the countless other things Jesus would be doing in my life.

> ***He united us into the very life of Christ.***
>
> **—Ephesians 2:5**

FREEDOM THEN VS. NOW

It's fun to think about the freedom I felt traveling as a nineteen-year-old, walking in wonderment amongst the white pillars of the Parthenon for the first time and the freedom I feel now as a fifty-five-year-old, hosting guests in my Airbnb from all over the world. I don't even recognize myself! The main difference is that now I don't have to run away from myself every day and start anew, hoping again tomorrow to find acceptance, connection, adventure, and peace, in spite of my own self-sabotage.

Hidden beneath my backpacking journey was a secret prison of not knowing who I was. Traveling was a way of running from the shame which was compelling me to move onto new places and people. If I ever saw the same people again in different places, my heart sunk. Assuming they didn't think highly of me, I made a slight but immediate withdrawal from them. At the time, this was manageable and was simply my normal life. I tried hard to be likable and continued along. I made friends, and on the outside, everything (no doubt) appeared great. But on the inside, I felt tight and constrained. I especially admired people who could freely express themselves in goofy and candid ways. Inside, I, too, desired the freedom to be whoever I was.

. . .

Today, I am in awe of what God has done in my life. I look people in the eye and delight in a relaxed and comfortable connection. I love who I am and invite others to share some of who they are with me, even if it's a momentary invitation to make themselves at home for their holiday. I am comfortable sharing deep emotions and happy to have nothing to hide. Walking the streets and smiling or chatting with strangers carries a special joy for me. I am amazed at how a simple exchange is so life-giving.

The other day, I met a young woman living on the street who I taught as a little girl. She recognized me, and her young eyes already spoke of pain and suffering. Before I knew it, I brought her into my arms and whispered to her about her value, acceptance, and safety in the Father's heart as she cried tears of sorrow. My heart broke in compassion as I walked away. I was thankful that I was free from self-awareness and able to truly connect with her. In connecting with the girl on the street, I know I also touched God's heart.

I barely recognize who I was at nineteen, and I smile at my spontaneity, my courage, and my desire to be goofy and candid. The journey to freedom has felt long and difficult yet totally worth every trouble to get here. I can't wait to look back on this time of life from the perspective of where the Father will take me next. I feel like life, in many ways, is just beginning.

TWO
UNRAVELLING

"Darling, everything is as it should be..."

"Whoever marries him will be a lucky woman," I thought to myself, gazing at Brian over my study notes. We had taken to occasionally studying together in the McLaren building at the University of Victoria. Usually, the conversation was peppered with controversial debates over topics such as the value of the United States of America versus Canada, and Brian and I were always on opposite sides. Yet, I saw that his loyalty and his good, steadfast heart would be a catch for someone to wake to every morning.

Months later, I had a dream I was in a wedding dress marrying Brian. This was a surprise, considering I was dating someone else. Several months later though, we began dating, and we were like two magnets of opposite force that couldn't separate. Brian was kind and considerate, always devoted to me, and soon became the love of my life. And I was his. We dated four years, including a wonderful year teaching in Japan together, where we were engaged. I didn't ever anticipate the roller coaster ride ahead, commonly called "marriage."

My first shock came the day after we were married. Brian had left our gift-opening party to visit his folks in their hotel because, unfortunately, his mom was quite sick at the time. I wished he had told me where he went. Alarmingly, a small communication issue soon turned into an axe-throwing hollering match with the both of us storming the beach where we were staying in the midnight hours and yelling I-don't-know-what at each other. Here, we had been thinking a private night on my parent's beach would be a romantic thing. The poor neighbors! Afterwards, we held each other in my mom and dad's small travel trailer, nurturing our hurting hearts. We laid there wondering what on earth had just happened.

We left on our honeymoon, so excited to be living together after spending a year teaching in Japan in nearby towns. In my rush and naiveté, I didn't bring any money for the trip. Having dated for four years, I foresaw no problem. However, from thirteen years old I had been earning my own money to buy my own clothes and spend as I liked. Packing for my honeymoon, I threw in my bathing suit, which was an old navy bikini I had bought in Italy for $5. No worries, I thought. I was excited to buy a new one in Hawaii. Looking through the many bathing suit shops, I finally found one I loved. To my dismay, when I asked Brian for money, he simply said no. It was too expensive, and I already had one. I shook my head in disbelief. Shock turned quickly to anger which turned to utter broken-heartedness. I was twenty-five years old, and, more than anything, I wanted a bathing suit that I could feel beautiful in for my husband. I expected him to want to care for my heart by giving me everything I wanted on my honeymoon. I didn't know what to think. To this day, I remember my honeymoon as tearful.

Wasn't marriage my answer to happiness?

Perhaps you've had similar misunderstandings in marriage. No one escapes the battle of two hearts forming into one. The yielding doesn't happen smoothly or easily, at least in my life.

One battle gave way to the next. Eventually, they seemed to fall into a rhythm of blaming and defending, each of us trying to protect our hearts. Certainly, I felt painful effects of anger and control which were Brian's way of handling his own fears. I would plead and pester to no avail.

As for my own coping strategies, perhaps they were acceptance and powerlessness, although it's funny how it is hard to see your own heart! I started off battling for control but ended up pretending to give up in order to keep the peace as much as possible. In retrospect, I had either a passive-aggressive or a victim mindset. What I held onto steadfastly was my dream of an intimate marriage, and, like a dancer, I moved the best I could, trying to step closer towards intimacy.

HELPLESSNESS

I hated yelling. Inside, it made me cringe and want to run for cover. I didn't understand how to navigate intense emotions and simply felt attacked with painful arrows. Perhaps it was the clutter of the diaper bag sitting in the hallway or kid's toys on the floor. I felt helpless and couldn't figure out what to do to defend myself or bring peace.

Friends would wonder why I didn't just pick up the clutter—problem solved! Yet, after several years of marriage, I believed that if I picked up the clutter, then the kitchen was too messy. If the kitchen was clean, then it was the coffee not made right. I just didn't have it in me to have two toddlers at home and a perfectly clean house. And if it wasn't housework, it was that I spent too much money. Anyway, I believed it went deeper than the clutter—certainly it was over my head to figure out. We couldn't spend a whole day together without anger ruining our peace.

I look back and think, yes, my husband was right on both counts: I could have kept a cleaner house, and I spent money much more freely than him. Furthermore, I can see that my passive, hopeless thinking was sadly rooted in powerlessness. Even at the time, I would agree with my husband on what he was upset about. I could see that, for his personality, these two issues would be a concern. He loved a clean house, and he didn't spend much money. The problem was not in his perception. He was right regarding what he wanted. The unfortunate part was that he didn't marry himself or someone like him, and forcing me to be like him was leading to disaster. Or was it? The pressure I was under was not helpful. Was it? Who was I anyway? Surely there must be space to live out our lives the way we want! Or is there? I didn't know what to do.

I AM ALIVE, BUT WHERE IS ABUNDANT LIFE?

The excitement of being married was merging into the reality of facing insecurities in my heart gradually being exposed. I was faced with Brian's control through anger when what I wanted most was peace and ultimately, love. Day in and day out, I struggled with the outpouring of hidden pain from my husband. Life was hard!

One thing I held onto was that in spite of his anger, Brian had a good heart. He was loyal, strong, and loving. Even when I would say, "I hate you," he would reply, "Well, I love you." And he meant it. I knew he would never leave me, and he was good at asking for forgiveness. However, life had done its damage to both of us, and now our brokenness was playing out in our marriage. Was this how a marriage was supposed to be?

Sadly, my heart was becoming exposed and raw. My own wounds widened and inadvertently invited more wounding. Our crazy cycle was painful and every aggressive encounter was like a knife entering my heart.

I found myself sobbing on my bed, shocked and confused about the argument we just had and the resulting pain I was feeling. This hurt more deeply than anything I had ever experienced in my life. The shattering of expectations of what I expected my marriage to be was devastating.

Around six or seven years into our marriage, I wondered if I even had it in me to continue the marriage. I remember pouring out my heart to my sister in tears. My weak button was someone being angry at me, especially since I needed my husband to love and hopefully romance me. The wind was knocked right out of me.

I continually worked towards intimacy in my relationship with Brian, but mostly what we both experienced was heartache. Thankfully, our relationship was peppered with moments of joy scattered throughout the year when we reconnected and found happiness for a time and especially with our children. But overall, I felt deflated and wondered what was God doing and where was the abundant life promised by Jesus? I began to come to Him with a simple call for help.

> ***Call to me and I will answer you and tell you great and unsearchable things you do not know.***
>
> **—Jeremiah 33:3, NIV**

Normally, I love to focus on the positive and what is giving me life. This was easy to do because my two young children were a joy, and being a mom filled my heart to overflowing. Our days were spent in fun activities and hanging out with friends. I have a large family that we connected with continually, and I drew strength from regular dinners and fun times gathering around a fire at my parent's beach. At a deep level, my heart was slowly learning that my happiness was never meant to depend on anyone except for God Himself. I transitioned gradually to depending on God for everything, and He became my lifeline, infusing hope into my spirit. I trusted Him to show me the way.

IT ONLY TAKES ONE!

The shattering of shame and insecurity came one step at a time by listening to my heart as the Holy Spirit led me. I'm so thankful for toddlers who are unaware of danger and walk where angels fear to tread.

One afternoon, in the middle of a loud argument with Brian, I remember little hands pulling my pants on each side of me, crying, "NO, NO, NO, NO, NO!" Their voices broke my heart. Seeing their distress led me to test the strategy that it takes two to fight, but usually, it only takes one to keep the peace. If I left the room or responded in peace, there was no one to fight with. Often, I found myself choosing whether I would respond to conflict in anger, which was tempting, or surrender my emotions completely to Jesus, trusting Him to take care of my heart. Thus began the rocky journey towards letting go of independence, my rights, and (ultimately) myself.

One battle at a time, I became dependent on God, which looked like silence and walking away in the beginning and crying to God about my sadness, leaving Him to defend me. I learned that the pathway to wholeness starts with a little light shining in the darkness.

I will admit that, at the time, it felt unfair for me to have to be the one to bend, but now I am so thankful I did. He began exposing my own insecurities, and everything felt like it got worse before He made any headway. This is why I call it my unraveling.

I refused to abandon hope for the romantic love I wanted in my marriage, especially since intimacy was like an ever-changing river. Inside of me, however, I was getting clarity on a deeper battle as well. This was something reflected in the goals for the new year I loved to make every January. One that stands out repeatedly was the desire to be free in my personality.

This underlying desire permeated all of my daily life. I felt locked in a prison, chained and lonely, lost in my personality and unsure of who I was. How wonderful it would have been to speak freely without feeling embarrassed about what I said! Self-doubt and insecurity plagued me, not overtly at home, but often in speaking with friends, co-workers, and certainly strangers.

The mystery of who I was felt unknown to me, and as a result, I felt constricted in most of my daily interactions. And, if anything, it was getting worse every year.

Whatever the revelation-light exposes, it will also correct, and everything that reveals truth is light to the soul.

—Ephesians 5:13

At some point, I began coming across the idea that what I believed about myself did not match up with what the Bible said. When I began inserting my name into the promises and declarations of how God thought of me, I was astonished at the gap. The verses about God's unfailing love and how He sees us as holy or pure just went over my head. The Holy Spirit began bringing to the surface what I believed about myself, such as, "I'm not interesting. People don't like me. God loves others, but I don't feel like He loves me. I'm not special. He died for the world in general but certainly not for me."

FAULTY FOUNDATION

I see now that a faulty foundation ends up tumbling the whole house, especially if there are earth tremors. The lies we believe simply won't hold us up well in turmoil. I was certainly in turmoil, and my foundation was shaking. I eventually learned that helplessness was one of my foundation stones, along with "less than" and other victim allies. Many lies that had been formed throughout my life and woven together in agreement, sat in lonely places in my heart.

While there are many effective strategies for conflict communication, my husband and I apparently knew few, if any of them. As a result, we continued wounding each other. So I poured out my heart to the Lord. Hidden bells clanging of unworthiness were beginning to come to the surface. Looking back, I realize now I displayed blazing signs, such as powerlessness, but at the time, my heart was still a mystery to me. Light was beginning to shine in these dark places that I didn't know existed. I started noticing other bad friends, such as impatience, anxiety, fear, and other forms of self-protection in me. Everything that He exposed in my heart widened the gap between how I saw myself and who the Bible said I was. Fortunately, God had a plan, which was already in play, beginning with His light shining on some of my brokenness.

> ***I pray that you will continually experience the immeasurable greatness of God's power made available to you through faith. Then your lives will be an advertisement of this immense power as it works through you!***
>
> **—Ephesians 1:19**

This was a powerful discovery for me. Paul's prayer in Ephesians was transformational: "I pray that you will **continually experience** the immeasurable greatness of God's power made available to you through faith." My pastor at the time, Pastor Dan, continually challenged me to live in the impossible power of God. He would preach about loving our enemies and even looking at people as if they were Jesus Himself. I understood that walking in love was the Christian life, no matter what, so there were times when I looked at Brian as if he was Jesus Himself standing in front of me. I spoke to him as if I was speaking to Jesus.

Standing on the promise of God's power always being available to me, when my heart was in pain, I learned to walk upstairs and close the door. I would sit in my rocking chair and cry out to Jesus: *I give You my hate! I let go of it the best I can. I need You to give me Your love for Brian because right now I don't have any left. And I'm not going back downstairs until You do.* Soon, peace and love would flood my heart where anger, hurt, and hatred had just been. I was amazed. I would walk down to the kitchen and continue preparing dinner. I could look at Brian and genuinely love him.

I NEED YOU TO BE MY SAFE PLACE

Another key in these years was continually reminding myself who Brian really was. I couldn't help but love his true self. This became my way of thinking about him, seeing beyond his actions into who God created him to be. Sometimes, I would communicate this: "I don't know what you're thinking right now, but that's not you." I'd say, "You are my husband that I trust to protect my heart and love me. I need you to be my safe place." This would melt away defensiveness and emotional safety returned. I treasured these moments and basked in our heart connection. Yet I found the road to reliable emotional security is surprisingly long.

Even after beautiful miracles and experiences in the Lord, it took quite a bit of courage for me to take a stand on how I wanted to be treated. When I came across the book, *Boundaries* by Henry Cloud, I felt both excited and nervous. I made a plan, and the opportunity soon came, to use it the next time Brian walked in the door upset. Standing in our bedroom door, I gathered my strength and said cooly, with unusual resolve, "I'm happy to talk with you when you're calm." And I walked past him. To my surprise, it was as easy as that! I wouldn't say that brought our hearts into intimacy, but it put a ceiling on the level of anxiety and conflict brought through emotional outbursts into our family.

Looking back, I see clearly that to the degree my heart was healed, I was able to hold space for respect, honor, and love to flow. Finding an alternative to loud outbursts was a stepping stone for us, and it signaled growing confidence in both our hearts, although the Father still had far more for us.

> ***He united us into the very life of Christ and saved us by his wonderful grace!***
>
> **—Ephesians 2:5**

Self-analyzing myself was a prison of its own. We are in Christ; that is our destination. We have arrived. In Him, we live and move and have our being. Our oneness with Him is an ever-increasing revelation, too incredible to express properly with words. However, at the time, this truth seemed to go over my head. That's the thing about revelation—when it comes, everything changes with a momentum of its own.

Meanwhile, I was always trying to improve myself, imagining that this would lead eventually to freedom. I believed that if I could die to my selfish nature and obey God in my new nature, then I would have arrived at living by the Spirit. Technically, since we have the Holy Spirit, I thought we should be able to live a perfect life, although I recognized I needed grace for mistakes. This achievement point of view based on my efforts pains me now to even write it out. I had not yet discovered what it meant to be one with Christ, in union with what He accomplished for me, knowing I am loved and accepted freely by the Father. It would be a long time before I discovered that my part is to let myself die, not try harder.

> ***We consider living to mean that we are constantly being handed over to death for Jesus' sake so that the life of Jesus will be revealed through our humanity.***
>
> **—2 Corinthians 4:11**

I prayed for the freedom to be myself for many years and had no idea that this was exactly what the Father was in the process of doing. The road looked confusing—a little longer, darker, and messier than I would have liked, but I dare not judge what was required for me to be able to stand in the freedom He had created me for. One thing is true, I was becoming more and more dependent on my relationship with Jesus to stay in peace and hope while waiting for my circumstances to change. He was my lifeline. His presence was my greatest comfort, and I trusted Him the best I could to lead me powerfully in my life and in all my relationships. I just didn't recognize that it was my heart that He was changing with every challenge that I faced.

CHRIST LIVES IN ME

I recall walking up the long, steep hill to my home, struggling to make Galatians 2:20 my reality. Over and over, I repeated to myself: *"I am crucified with Christ and I no longer live, but Christ lives in me. I am crucified with Christ and I no longer live..."* I was seeing that all of my brokenness—vulnerability, the pain of feeling misunderstood, not being valued and seen as I would have hoped, desiring to be cherished and adored no matter what— was in process of being placed on the cross with Jesus.

I see now that the nails of the cross crucified me, as well as Jesus. Every time I let go of a desire, it was a surrender of self, even like a death to what I wanted at the moment. Letting go of the pain of desiring to be adored and treated as special was hard. I felt like I was giving up my rights. Letting go is like dying. I thought of it as my old nature that I needed to let go of. I wanted it all exposed in the light so that my Father could bring healing.

My understanding of what happened on the cross and in the resurrection was vague in those days, but it was enough to chip away at my idol of self and allow suffering to shape me. Letting go of what I wanted and allowing the reality of what was to play out in my life was a long process. However, my relationship with Jesus was growing quickly. Allowing old memories or present-day pain to be brought into the light, where we are one with Jesus on the cross, is a privilege and the answer to our longing for freedom. Dying on the cross with Him to the emotions in my heart was the key. Here, He won the victory over all darkness.

> ***Let me make this clear: A single grain of wheat will never be more than a single grain of wheat unless it drops into the ground and dies. Because then it sprouts and produces a great harvest of wheat—all because one grain died.***
>
> **—John 12:24**

Who was the grain of wheat who fell into the ground and died? The grain of wheat was Jesus. There is only one grain of wheat, Brian Simmons explains.[1] And amazingly, we are one with

Him. His death is our death. Unless the grain of wheat dies, it doesn't sprout up into a beautiful harvest.

This is my story, experiencing the pain of being crushed as a grain of wheat. There is a place of death, which is a form of suffering and eventually letting go of our pain, letting go of control, and completely surrendering our hearts to Jesus. We may not recognize our spirit is experiencing light shining on darkness. Often, I didn't like what I saw. It's hard to believe how selfish my heart looked and how much I just wanted to be loved. Jesus won the victory over my battles and suffered my losses. He knew the way. Thankfully, the light had come for my healing so that I could also stop inflicting pain on the people I loved. Holy Spirit, open the eyes of our heart to Jesus' light, so that we may receive healing.

> ***And now the essence of this new life is no longer mine, for the Anointed One lives his life through me—we live in union as one! My new life is empowered by the faith of the Son of God who loves me so much that he gave himself for me, and dispenses his life into mine!***
>
> **—Galatians 2:20**

What would I say to my young married self?

> We are one with the most powerful force in the universe, the Lord Himself. You are on a journey of discovery into the secret places of your soul where the Father is bringing His love. Life is found here, in the hidden chambers of your heart. The Lord has come and

made His home there. He is comfortable living amongst the deepest parts of who you are. He is pouring His love into your sore spots right now. He accepts your whole self. Let go of the process and trust Him to father you. You don't have to be healed or perfect, but rather, He wants you to come to Him with all your brokenness and let Him love you there. He is not afraid of your mistakes. In fact, Jesus died for them, and they are not a barrier to the Holy Spirit. These are the places to invite Him into.

Try not to judge the people who hurt you, especially your family. Let people have their own journey of mistakes and failures. You are stronger than you know and you are certainly not helpless. As you invite love in, your heart will be transformed into a creative, life flowing force that will speak gentle wisdom and encouragement to those around you. You know much less than you think, so let go of what you think you know. Love is the only thing that matters.

Enjoy the journey. Be weak, be messy, be authentic all along the way. Life is not about getting things right. It's about staying connected and accepting each other the way we are. Living with your heart wide open will inspire others to do the same. Be a safe place for others. Don't tell anyone what they should do. The Father's job is to do that. Your job is to be gentle with your heart, to be loved by God, and communicate vulnerably and clearly. Stand your ground for what you need and let go of how you think things should look. Nothing is that fun or important that you need to go to. Focus on your priorities—love God and love your people, including yourself—and everything else will fall into place. Be patient. You are loved.

PRAYER

Holy Spirit, open the eyes of my heart to Jesus' light so that I may receive healing. Help me to hand my sadness, the way others see me, and the pain in my heart to You right now. I choose to let them go the best I can. I am one with You, Jesus, surrendered to who You are in me. I am one with You while You are on the cross, and I am one with You in Your resurrection. I sit with You in heavenly places and rest in who You are. Thank You, Jesus, for all You have done out of Your love for me. Amen.

THREE
WILDERNESS

He will care for you
as a shepherd tends his flock,
gathering the weak lambs and taking
them in his arms. He carries them close
to his heart and gently leads
those that have young.
—Isaiah 40:11—

They say that the wilderness is a time for receiving revelation. To me, it was a heart-wrenching battle with self-condemnation and hidden judgment, with pockets of miraculous glory worth everything. I would call it a roller coaster, except my heart was steadfastly straining upwards and trying to pull my marriage along with it. I identified with Paul when he stated, ***"I run the race with perseverance" (Hebrews 12:1)***.

Lost and wandering in a circle, repeatedly fighting the same battles, I wondered, "Will I ever be free?" While I am gentle and kind to myself now, I was not patient. I still had much to discover about who the Father was for me and who I really was. Sadly, in these years, I was tangled in a web of self-condemnation, while continually seeking the road to inner peace. Yikes, when I consider how I used to talk to myself, feeling guilty about everything—I'm not eager to go back there! My comfort lifelines were stripped away, and I felt trapped in whatever was hidden in my heart. But if anyone else would be set free from self-criticism and judgment stemming from unworthiness and a sense of shame, then I run back with joy to share how the Lord has set me free.

> ***Let me be clear, the Anointed One has set us free—not partially, but completely and wonderfully free! We must always cherish this truth and stubbornly refuse to go back into the bondage of our past.***
>
> **—Galatians 5:1**

It was summer holidays again and the kids were excited to visit Grandma and Grandpa and their cousins on Vancouver Island. Bursting through the door, with hugs all round, they were excited to even find wrapped gifts on their pillows. My in-laws were wonderful, accepted me into the family with love, and I loved them in return. Yet inside of me, there was a tension that I didn't understand until much later. All I knew was within hours of arrival, I started to feel a familiar stress clenching my inner self until I became exhausted with a headache, soon accompanied by nausea and low energy.

I could tell I felt insecure but for no rational reason. I sensed the differences in our family mindsets, and I didn't know how to maneuver freely in giving and receiving acceptance for our differences. My stomach would drop at imagined perceptions because insecurity had such a hold on me. For a decade, I didn't call my mother-in-law anything because she said I could call her Mom or her name, whichever I wanted. I wanted to call her Mom but needed reassurance that she wanted that, too. My husband was close to his family and was delighted to be home. As for me, I loved them too, but struggled with not knowing how to be myself around anyone.

One year in the spring, I was puttering in my kitchen, and I had the thought: *memorize Romans 8*. Surprised, I read it through and absolutely loved its comfort and reassurance. I had been so caught up in Romans 7, in the frustration of going in circles with what it said about not doing what I want to do and doing what I don't want to do. When I landed on Romans 8, I was completely and joyously taken aback.

> ***There is now no condemnation for those who are in Christ Jesus ..the mind governed by the Spirit is life and peace.. the Spirit you received brought about your adoption to sonship. And by Him we cry, "Abba, Father." The Spirit himself testifies with our spirit that we are God's children. In the same way, the Spirit helps us in our weakness. ..If God is for us, who can be against us? Who shall separate us from the love of Christ? Shall trouble or hardship or persecution or famine or nakedness or danger or sword?. No, in all***

> ***these things we are more than conquerors through him who loved us.***
>
> **—Romans 8:1-38, NIV**

GIFT OF REVELATION

Every morning, I came to the Lord with my Bible opened to Romans chapter eight. I memorized 2 verses a day, always reviewing from the beginning so as not to forget. Even if it wasn't perfect at first, with the review every day, I soon memorized the whole chapter of 38 verses. It was almost as if God was downloading it all into me as a gift because it seemed unusually easy to memorize. It took me about 10 minutes to recite the whole chapter aloud. The beauty of it was, each day, the promises in Romans 8 would sink deeper. Clarity unfolded in my spirit, and soon I was basking in the glory of the revelation of these life-giving promises. Verses that were over my head at first slowly became part of who I was. To this day, it is one of my favorite chapters in the Bible.

That summer when we went on our yearly family holiday, Romans 8 spoke peace to my inner demons. Every time I started to feel that crazy tension, based on nothing that I understood, I started to recite Romans 8 in my head.

Often, I found a reason to drive somewhere in the car and say it out loud. Within 10 minutes, as I got to the end of the chapter where nothing could separate me from the love of Christ, I was calm and relaxed again. I did this several times a day! This was a most exciting breakthrough, and for a couple of years, Romans 8 was my constant companion. This wasn't just family tension I experienced; it was actually everywhere I went. But His word spoke life into my spirit, and I received it like oxygen to my soul. Phew! My head was above water but I still had a long way to freedom.

> ***Those who look to him are radiant; their faces are never covered with shame.***
>
> **—Psalm 34:5**

Underneath a friendly but sometimes cool demeanor, I wore a subtle cloak of shame and unworthiness. They were close friends with judgment and condemnation. I even wrote the above scripture on a little bench I made, drawing comfort from the Holy Spirit.

One of my repetitive dreams involved dark connections with spider web strands that were impossible to be free from. At least that's what it felt like. I was not a perfectionist in outward tasks, however, when it came to trying my best and doing things with excellence, I was a prisoner to self-judgment. I could always try harder and do better. A list of lies kept me chained and feeling suffocated. Of course, I was the hardest on myself, but in my gentle but firm way, I also encouraged and expected excellence from those around me, like my children and my students.

This worked itself out in good ways as well. Interestingly, children have a natural tendency towards trying their best and love to be encouraged in that direction. I discovered they can accomplish much more than most people imagine. Motivation births inspiration and excitement to learn. I'm all for producing fabulous work in creative and healthy ways and loved watching my children grow in astounding leaps and bounds, which built confidence. Learning is exciting and it is impossible to be bored when the brain is engaged in active learning. I think that in spite of our weaknesses, God still uses us in beautiful ways.

As I look back on my journey, I find that God worked many glorious things out of an imperfect me. This reminds me that our brokenness is not a hindrance to God. Actually, it is normal and *everything really is as it should be*, as much as I want to hurry the process. If only I could have believed earlier that I was accepted as I was! I know now that we are right where we need to be because He is leading our journey. We don't need to fret or beat ourselves up. Helene King says, "What if we offered grace and peace to ourselves every time we messed up?"[1] Isn't this what Jesus does? The Father was proud of me in the middle of my insecurities, my great efforts, and mixed up motivations because He was teaching me everything in His timing. My heart and your heart are the focus of His attention.

WHERE DO WE GET OUR VALUE?

My primary value was clearly in achievement and what everyone else thought about me. I constantly was assessing right/wrong, better/worse, and good/bad. Remember, this was my time of wandering through the wilderness, completely lost for years but still receiving incredible discoveries here and there.

The presence of God would fill me on occasion, and I would be in awe, so thankful the whole day. His encouragement kept me going, and I loved my Christian life. I continued growing in Him for many years, depending on Him but also praying for Him to reveal His tangible love for me. Still, I had no understanding that Father was the one fathering me—I thought it was my pressing in and striving for excellence that caused Him to give me revelations. Sometimes now, I try to imagine His perspective, watching me learn, grow, and discover. I may think I know something, but I fall, cry, and learn it all over again. I imagine His eyes are full of love and gentleness, without a thought for my perceived failures, but delighted to watch my steps.

One morning, some years after becoming a Christian and striving continually to be the best Christian/mom/teacher/wife/friend/person I could be, I woke with a clear thought. I recognized my especially clear thoughts upon waking as being from the Lord. It was "I desire mercy, not sacrifice." This was a turning point for me. That morning I painted a picture of a hungry mouse who had stolen cheese, and the other mice loaded his plate with more cheese out of mercy. I knew intuitively I was to take my hand off the wheel and not worry about other people's lives. I hadn't realized I was thinking that all my striving somehow made me better qualified than someone else. It's likely that I had it completely backward and also upside down, but I hadn't yet understood what it means to be a daughter. That would come much later. For now, I began looking at everyone as someone God loved and began letting go of my idea of what everyone else should be. I'm sure this was a relief to my family in particular, but again, the complete transformation had some deep roots to be pulled over time.

My wilderness journey was about discovering what matters to God. The first time I came across the scripture, *"The only thing that matters is faith expressing itself in love,"* (Gal. 5:6), I was shocked. Surely wisdom matters! What about great things like excellence, character, courage, morality, worship, and hard work? Slowly, I began to understand that He meant what He said. Nothing matters except love to God. He is love. Living in Him is living in love. Everything else is filtered through love. If it's not filtered through love, He doesn't value it because He always looks at the heart.

UNRAVELING HEART ISSUES THROUGH MY CAREER

When my children were still toddlers, I began to teach part-time again. I hated to leave them, but I also loved teaching children and found I was excellent at it, despite my first year of being eaten alive by my students. With a second chance, no seven year old was going to get the best of me again and it turned out that I flourished in the classroom. However, the Father was on the move, unraveling me in another area of my heart.

With school enrollment declining, jobs were scarce and schools were closing. Every term position I was hired for ended with no assurance for the next year. I interviewed for multiple positions, some for which I was hired and others I wasn't chosen. I was heartbroken whenever I wasn't chosen and also, at year-end, with no job for the fall. Everyone was planning for next year's classes, while I forlornly packed up my desk.

Countless times, I struggled with rejection and receiving value from my status as a teacher. I wrestled with the Lord until gradually, my heart was less impacted by my job status. Right after this period, Father launched me into the career position of my dreams.

It began with the prayer of Jabez, prayed earnestly from my heart:

> ***Oh, that You would bless me indeed, and enlarge my territory, that Your hand would***

be with me, and that You would keep me from evil, that I may not cause pain.

—1 Chronicles 4:9-10, KJV

After ten years of teaching in the public school, I had been longing in my heart to be able to teach in a Christian environment where I could teach and share the most important thing in my heart, which was Jesus, and weave Bible truths in anytime. In March 2003, my whole world was rocked. I was walking with my friend, Linda, on an ordinary spring day. She was also a member of the Christian school board. She calmly said, "We want you to come and be the principal and a teacher of our new Christian school." Astounded, my heart leaped out of my chest. This was surely my dream!

However, my husband would have none of it. He fought for the rights of public school teachers and private schools were considered the enemy—besides, the pay was too low with no benefits. My faith remained resolute, and I waited for the Lord. I opened my Bible after standing my ground one time against Brian for the dream job of my life, and these words jumped off the page: your faith will be richly rewarded. From that moment, I simply waited expectantly. Soon enough, my husband's job was cut, and he said that I would have to take the offer at the Christian school. My excitement could not be contained.

Miracles soon became the norm, with supplies and specific needs brought in every day. My to-do list was pages long, and yet I worked tirelessly with extraordinary strength and wisdom, not only in setting up the school, but through its groundbreaking first year. I was the Principal, a teacher of 4 grades—Kindergarten through 3rd Grade—with 22 students, and simultaneously, secretary for half the day. I would flop into bed each night, my heart bursting with joy. "I poured myself out for you today, Lord," I would smile into my pillow. I knew I was born for this.

My ten years of anguish in going from job to job had perfectly prepared me for being the principal and teacher of multiple grades. I confidently handled any issue that arose. I had taught learning assistance, ESL, special needs, split grade classes, every grade, and every elementary school subject. I had experience with wealthy families, and the expectations they had were similar to a private school. Suddenly, I understood that I hadn't been devalued with each different position I moved to, I was being carefully *prepared* for a challenging assignment. I was in awe of how God works, and I learned to stop judging whether something was good or bad based on what I know, want, or even feel like I need. This discovery resulted in holding my judgments of situations more loosely and has been an important step in living in freedom, living flexibly, and adapting to life events. Really, it's just trusting my Father with my life.

I am overflowing with love for God as I remember what He did in this year. To my delight, my daughter was in my class, which warmed my heart to no end. I watched my son gather the whole school on the playground to play 'Capture the Flag' during recess. I knew that since I was in the middle of the Lord's will, He would meet my family's needs, given the long hours I worked.

My heart was still in anguish over my husband's continued conflict with me working at a private school in spite of him telling me to take the job, but the Lord was also teaching me to stand. I didn't always stand well; it was a mixture of success and failure really. But at the end of the year, I knew it had gone on long enough, and I was able to communicate the needless pain he was causing in a strength and vulnerability that Brian finally understood. He responded with sorrow, and we never looked back. I now see that he also was looking for a way to communicate his own fears which were legitimate around pay, time, and pension. We were imperfect in our understanding of each other, but I'm amazed at how much room there is in God's heart for our mistakes. It's limitless, really.

FAILURE

Tragically, my supernatural joy ended near the end of the school year when our out-of-town superintendent came to visit. He asked me if I preferred teaching or being a principal. With working twelve hours a day, six or seven days a week, I knew that, as a mom, an adjustment needed to be made for next year. In my heart, I knew that being the principal of the school was what truly made my heart sing. The joy I experienced every day was beyond what even I had dreamed of. Teaching in combination with allowing creativity to flow in all aspects of school life as a whole was where I felt God's powerful anointing to face every challenge, even in spite of severe opposition. But I still couldn't truthfully answer a simple question because I believed it would be thinking too highly of myself. I responded, "Teaching." I expected him to know my heart and give me more time in my schedule to do principal duties. Big mistake. I didn't have the confidence or the courage to be honest, and in the blink of an eye, my dream was shattered.

I cried to the Lord most mornings for the next two years. I shared my heart with him mournfully. I regretted how I responded and couldn't accept not being in charge of the school, even though I also found joy in my classroom. "It is not your time," God told me twice. Steadfastly, I still poured myself into supporting the school and eventually let go of disappointment with grace for myself and the people involved.

The pain of living my dream in the Spirit and then having it taken away due to lack of confidence is a pain I never want to go through again. I resolved in the next opportunity to live authentically with courage. Meanwhile, the Lord was working on exposing those roots and making me stronger and freer in who I was born to be.

BLESSED AND IN HIS FAVOR

> ***Every spiritual blessing in the heavenly realm has already been lavished as a love gift from our wonderful heavenly Father, the Father of our Lord Jesus - all because He sees us wrapped into Christ.***
>
> **—Ephesians 1:3**

My early morning quiet times with the Lord were my strength and my peace. I told Him of my personal concerns and desires and listened to His responses. His words and presence encouraged me, but there was one breathtaking discovery that stood out. Through a Beth Moore Bible study, I learned that blessings given by God are as strong as a covenant, which lasts forever. My discovery was that God does not change His mind depending on my behavior.[2]

When Isaac was tricked into blessing Jacob instead of Esau, it could not be undone. When Jacob crossed his hands in blessing his grandsons, Ephraim and Manasseh, it was irreversible. Therefore, in the new covenant, when it says we too are blessed and in God's favor, absolutely nothing we do can change that. I was elated. Excitement coursed through me in waves of relief! I was blessed by God and in His favor!

The joy that this revelation sparked in my heart made way for something new. Taking me way out of my comfort zone, in worship, I found my arms danced—it seemed of their own will —to express the love for God in my heart, and BOOM! I was supernaturally brought so high and so close to the Father that I experienced a beautiful, aching, almost painful encounter, but in the best way. Incredibly, I was overcome by the intensity of His love and the power of His presence. I could only stand it for a few short moments before I pulled back. Immediately, I was filled with desperation to be back in His presence again.

This happened four or five times, each equally or more intense than the previous, over a month or so. Every time I could stand to be in the intensity of His love only a few seconds before withdrawing, wishing only to return! This simple movement of allowing my arms to float high in worship brought a life-changing encounter of a love more powerful than my heart could contain. Somehow this broke a barrier for me in what others might think of me dancing with my hands, something I would normally have been horrified to do at the time. It's also interesting how the Father was showing me that what we have faith for, He honors, and even more than we ask or imagine. Soak in His promise:

> ***Never doubt** God's mighty power to work in you and accomplish all this. He will achieve infinitely more than your greatest request,*

> ***your most unbelievable dream, and exceed your wildest imagination! He will outdo them all, for his miraculous power constantly energizes you.***
>
> **—Ephesians 3:20**

After this experience, I prayed for God to let me share my joy with others. In answer, I soon received a phone call asking if I would lead a women's retreat in the spring on the topic of joy. My heart leaped, knowing this was my opportunity. I told God that I would be happy to speak, but it would be His job to ensure I wasn't nervous so that I could speak in a relaxed, cheerful way that released joy.

To my amazement, for the first time ever, I couldn't have been more peaceful in front of a crowd. When I began speaking, I didn't once look at my notes and I felt a special bubble of His presence surround me the entire time. I also didn't realize the significance that the word joy would be bringing into my life seven years later.

I WOULD LIKE to share with you my heartfelt journal entry from this season, expressing my joy and who He was for me:

December 24, 2006

> *The Lord is my Redeemer*
> *Giving me life itself*
> *The Lord gives me freedom*
> *And His favor rests upon me.*

His blessings are binding
His gifts are eternal
He has taken my heart of clay
And molded it for his desires.

I am Yours, declares His child
Only You can unbind my tangled soul.
You alone give me wings to soar beyond myself.
Your Spirit is life to me.

You have given me a new name,
I know it; I feel it.
Your Spirit draws me to Yourself
Oh, to be in favor with THE LORD*!*

He sees me and lifts my soul up,
He fills me with His Glory.
Keep me near to You, my Father,
And teach me Your ways.

My sins are washed away;
My heart is clean
Your blood is my salvation
Your holiness is my light.

Spirit of God, fill me;
I believe Your word and accept Your discipline,
A taste of Your freedom
Has filled me with completeness.

I long to bless,
To share this joy with others;
Your works are laid out for me

Since time began.

Spirit of God, move in me,
Spread faith and freedom to Your people
Do not let me hold myself back,
But may your power give flight to many nearby.

I love You, my King—my Christmas hope!

FOUR
FAITH

"Now, think of the happiest things. It's the same as having wings."[1]
—Peter Pan—

Faith has been my biggest battle. It's one thing to have faith in God, but it's another challenge to believe He will come into my failures and weaknesses. Faith has almost become synonymous with courage to me. It takes courage to believe in His love for me—to step courageously out onto the water and leave behind what I felt were my rights and certainly my desires. Faith looked like coming to God in the mornings and asking Him to lead me in prayer as I opened my heart to Him. Faith was inviting Him to fill me, guide me, and lead me to let go of my daily troubles, and to trust His love and goodness. I would ask for His protection and for Him to lay out all the details of my life. In this way, my heart connected with His. In the supernatural, I had begun to discover meaningful life in my relationship with Jesus. His peace gave me a taste of freedom which only made me long for more.

MIGRAINE HEALING

I have a tendency to focus on the positive and not really acknowledge difficulties, or at least the extent of them, until I am on the other side. I love this strategy because it enables me to enjoy my days in relative peace while trusting God for victory. In these days of being a young mom and living out my struggles for a warm, life-giving marriage, the presence of God was my lifeline. While I didn't experience Him as often as I wanted, the wait was so worth it. My battle with feeling "less than" still hadn't budged over the years, and by this time, I am spending three days in a row recovering from migraine headaches that make it extremely difficult to look after my two incredible children. My bold and spunky daughter, Jenna, filled my heart with love. I was in awe of her 3-year-old exuberant joy. Brett was an adorably thoughtful and creative presence that breathed life into everyone.

From my mid-twenties, I began having increasingly worse pre-migraine headaches. They began with nausea and eventually incapacitated me for several days. I lived like this for ten years, surviving about half the time on extra-strength Tylenol, a triple dose every four hours. Knowing I couldn't look after my children with migraine headaches, I gathered my kiddos, told them to put their hands on Mommy's head and pray for her headache to go away. Promptly, little earnest voices echoed in my ears. At this point, the only healing I had seen was in the Bible, but I stood up believing I was healed. Within ten minutes, I noticed my headache and nausea were miraculously gone! Shocked and excited, I was beside myself with incredulity. I knew this was a turning point for me, and I determined at once to take no more medications for headaches.

Days later, I felt the familiar stomach-turning nausea, and I instinctively knew that stress over something silly I had said must be the cause. Not aware of what it was, I asked God to show me the root of my headache. A faint memory came into my mind of something I had said in the previous couple of days. I simply said to the Lord, "I give this to you. My words, what people think about me, and the headache, too." Immediately, I stepped away from the place where I was standing, thinking I was leaving my headache there in God's hands, and in faith, I trusted Him for healing. Again, within minutes, I was light and free from pain! My head was clear, and I was ecstatic!

This began a cycle beginning with feeling the familiar nausea in my stomach as the headache began. As soon as possible, I found a quiet spot to open my heart to God. I asked Him what was causing me stress. A memory would come to mind, usually a recent conversation where I felt insecure. I would let it all go into His hands, pray for my headache to be healed, and stand up in faith as if it was. Every single time, I was healed. The time in between headaches beginning was also increasing until soon it was six months, then a year, and now, thanks to God, it has been over twenty-four years without a headache.

This experience increased my faith for further healing. I had discovered that a similar thing happened with colds or cases of flu. So I began praying at the beginning of cold symptoms coming on. Astonishingly, I was healed! In fact, I didn't have one cold or flu after this point the entire time I was a teacher, even as the flu would sweep through my school, time and again. I have noticed that some people have minimized healing from having a cold or flu, but I was amazed and overflowing with joy each time I discovered God as my Healer.

SPIRITUAL OPPOSITION

My time being the principal of the Christian school had ruined me for ordinary life. My heart loved being stretched beyond what anyone could possibly do on their own, and I thrived in being launched into complete dependence on God. This was life for me. Living in the Spirit had a flow of supernatural strength where there seemed to be limitless energy. However, living in this place also brought spiritual opposition.

In the first year of opening the Christian school, there were many strange occurrences that I attributed to darkness trying to interfere with what God was doing. Each time, I would fight back with spiritual force.

> ***Be well balanced and always alert, because your enemy, the devil, roams around incessantly, like a roaring lion looking for its prey to devour. Take a decisive stand against him and resist his every attack with strong, vigorous faith.***
>
> **—1 Peter 5:8-9**

One morning in the middle of the year, I woke up clear-minded and rested. I was interacting happily with my husband. I went into the bathroom, and the next thing I know, I woke up on the floor, having fainted. This had never happened before.

When I opened my eyes, I was so sick I could barely move. I certainly couldn't speak. Head over the toilet, I prayed without words for God to heal me. I reminded Him how He had brought me to this school. I mentioned that no one could manage the range of children and all the activities I had planned for them that day as I could. It would be complete chaos, and it was unreasonable to ask that of someone. I told God, "I need to go to work." I glanced at my reflection in a mirror and noticed that my face had a blue tinge. I felt so sick that I thought, "Oh, this is how people die from the flu!" I had never been even close to this sick, where I couldn't move.

My husband was speaking on the phone asking a teacher if she would substitute for me. I suddenly felt my foggy head clearing and energy starting to flow in my body. I heard myself say, "No, I'm fine, I'm actually healed now." I stood up and took the phone from my confused husband. Amazingly, all that remained was a quality of feeling wiped, like I'd been through the wringer, but now I was on the other side. I went to work that day, and thanks to my Healer, I had a great day.

Each time I dealt with a spiritual attack, my confidence in God rose as I watched how He would save me. One time later in the year, shooting pains in my jaw became almost terrifying. The first several days, I froze in place, gripped my cheeks and closed my eyes until the pain passed within a few moments. Often, this was in my classroom, and my young students watched in wide-eyed silence.

I went to the dentist, and he told me I needed a major procedure. By the weekend, I was feeling deflated and slightly traumatized by the toll the pains were taking on me. I am so thankful for Pastor Jim. After I told him what was happening, he immediately trusted God for healing, took authority over demonic interference, and forbade it to return. That was the end of that. I excitedly shared this story with my dentist, but he told me my pain would definitely return. Thanks to God, seventeen years later, it still hasn't returned.

FASTING

Every time we step out in faith, we are positioned for new revelation, new experiences, and new healing. I've heard it described as levels of faith. This is not something I can manufacture, but I can take the opportunities God has put in front of me. Often, these have come to me in the form of a clear thought, although sometimes fairly faint.

I was praying for one of my teenagers because I was concerned about a decision they were making. I certainly didn't want to get in a power struggle with them. I believed in living life with opportunities to make mistakes in the safety of being at home and growing up. The thought came into my mind to begin a fast. Immediately, I reacted enthusiastically, "Can I fast, Lord?! Can I fast for 40 days?!"

Now, I had never fasted and didn't even know if a person could survive 40 days on juice. However, I sensed the thought was from the Lord, and here began an incredible journey with indescribable blessings. First, I asked Him for the name of my fast. He said, "Fast for intimacy with Me." Wow. I began with using my intuition, vegetable/fruit juice fasting (with no chewing at all), and avoiding sugar and dairy.

First of all, I simply listened intently to the Lord. He began by telling me to empty myself. For a whole two weeks, every day I would lay down everything that came to mind: my past, my marriage, my children and husband, friends, work, future, dreams, and so on. Every time I thought of food, I lifted up a prayer for what brought me to the fast, although it was now primarily about intimacy with Jesus. I came into a rhythm of juicing in the morning, smoothies in the evening, and drinking lots of water. I was so curious about how my body would handle this routine. I seemed to be okay! I didn't appear to be dying. My mind became crystal clear. Shockingly, even my voice seemed to carry a broader range and singing became easier. Old scars healed completely, stomach issues resolved, stiffness in my feet went away, and my hair stopped falling out when I washed it. I began to grow in energy and needed much less sleep than usual. At nine o'clock at night, instead of reading in bed, I was now making cookies for my family. If I couldn't eat, at least I could delight in cooking delicious food for everyone else. I had never felt so good, after the initial few days, and especially in the last twenty days.

> ***This means that God is transforming each one of you into the Holy of Holies, his dwelling place, through the power of the Holy Spirit living in you!***
>
> **—Ephesians 2:22**

As the weeks wore on, I felt so filled with the Holy Spirit that my breath was taken away. I remember praying one time for our church service, asking for the pastor to invite the congregation to share what God was doing in them this week. It happened exactly as I prayed, word for word out of his mouth, with a real and vulnerable sharing time. I remember crying as the fast was drawing near to an end because I had never experienced such glory, resting in God's presence.

I never told anyone the reason I had started fasting in the first place. I felt I was to keep it quiet and let God work, without any manipulation on my part. On day thirty-five, one of my children shared with me their new decision. Surprised and delighted, I asked why they had decided this. The answer was simply, "Because God told me to." In all of my life, I don't know that I have ever felt so in awe of how God works. My heart flooded with love for Him in return. This forty day fast was a purifying of my faith and an invitation to go deeper, with countless small miracles and an intimate time of shared communion. My response was a heart full of worship where I certainly did not want to leave His presence nor end the fast. After not eating for so long, it was satisfying to eat, but it was also somewhat of a disappointment in comparison to the fullness of the Spirit that I had come to love so much. I don't even remember my first meal.

By this time, family life had developed a rhythm, I was relying on God for emotional strength, and there was an increasing amount of peace between my husband and I. We loved to travel, and once we found our stride, we never stopped. After the first year of teaching at the Christian school, we went to Europe for five weeks. I saw this as a gift from God. We had interviewed for and were offered teaching positions in England, but I took the opportunity at the Christian school instead.

We were accepted to house sit in a lovely doctor's home in Buckinghamshire. Apparently, in England, they didn't leave their homes vacant while on holiday. Actually, the real story is that I went to England in a wheelchair, due to extreme sciatic nerve pain that I was experiencing at the end of my school year. Many things happened that year! Against medical advice, I went to Europe with confidence, believing this was a gift from God. Anyways, I thought I could sit in a home in a lovely

English village just as well as in my home in Canada. It turns out that in England they advise lots of walking for sciatic pain. Excited to munch on fish and chips, along with their famous mushy peas, we walked along happily in the unusual summer heatwave of 2014 along the cobbled streets, resting in a local theatre for an afternoon live show of *Jungle Book*. With the help of my crutches, extensive stretching, walking every day, and acupuncture treatment by an old Chinese woman, I was fully healed in a month—an awesome miracle, considering my chiropractor said it would take a solid 6 months.

In the meantime, our family enjoyed incredible sightseeing and quality time with each other after an unusually busy year. This trip made us realize we could find ways to travel without a lot of money. Most importantly, the value of connecting with each other, having great fun, taking new risks, and also allowing time for proper communication and heart issues to resolve was worth everything. Flowing in the Spirit by following our hearts in this case was a life-changer for our family.

GET READY

Two years later, our family decided to go to Italy, Greece, and Turkey. It was an incredible adventure, full of highs and inevitable bumps. The great thing about being together with my family for a month was that it was impossible to hide how we were feeling. Emotions released in the most inopportune moments. However, because everyone around was speaking a different language, it gave the illusion of a safe zone.

This is what it was like during Ramadan in Istanbul in Sultanahmet Square near the blue mosque. Families had traveled far and wide to celebrate in the colorful capital city. Istanbul is a picturesque place, like in the movie Aladdin, surrounded by Turkish style peaked domes and lively vendors, with the smell of kabobs and fresh pomegranate juice everywhere. Women wearing their hijab or burka would be rolling fresh flatbread behind store windows. Turkish cafes invited you to lounge in billowy cushions and rest in comfy sofas with hookahs boasting every flavor of tobacco, such as apple or mint. Families spread out their evening feasts on tablecloths on the grass after fasting all day.

In the midst of this commotion, one day my heart was bursting with unresolved pain as my husband and I tried to maneuver a disagreement, no doubt rooted in years of hurting each other in the same area. Amidst tears and the flurry of the Muslim crowds, our hearts were laid out bare, unable to be silenced any longer. I discovered that it doesn't matter exactly how I express myself, when it comes from within, everyone knows. Urgency, or perhaps even budding confidence, started to emerge, knowing that I needed to be heard, and I wasn't backing down. I remember my teenagers wondering at my insistence and even reluctance to forgive until I felt understood. I kind of liked the openness to freely communicate in the bustling foreign atmosphere. Speaking honestly created vulnerability. Combined with lots of time, issues worked themselves out, breathing life into all of our family relationships.

What I remember most about Turkey was the catalyst for my next season, one of the most spectacular journeys in the Spirit I was yet to know. Something seemingly terrible set off the course of events. My daughter, Jenna, and I had used blankets in a hostel in Venice that caused us to break out in itchy patches all over our skin. Hers developed into a horrible secondary infection on her legs that we didn't realize the severity of. While staying at our bed and breakfast near the spice market, a medical student working there noticed what was going on. Amazingly, he and the owner of the little hotel helped Jenna with what she needed, including a massive needle behind a curtain in the crowded pharmacy. Amidst servings of apple tea and Turkish coffee, the beginnings of a friendship was sparked with this hotel worker. I thought I heard God say, "Pray for him."

Upon returning to Canada, I obediently prayed for our new Muslim friend. I went into travail, emotionally crying in prayer, which was fairly new for me as I felt Jesus' heart to reveal Himself to him. The whole situation was unfamiliar for me, and I struggled with faith to believe I'd heard God correctly. After all, through Facebook messages, he was at the same time asking permission to date and marry my daughter. Several weeks of waffling later, my sister Deanna was listening to my doubt about whether God had asked me to pray for him. She challenged me, saying, "Either it's of God or it isn't. If it is, believe, and if not, just let it go. But make up your mind."

WALKING ON AIR

I gathered up my evidence and decided that it had to be God, but it was still the hardest thing I ever had to believe. So, together, we prayed: *God, show me how to have faith.* Immediately, I saw an airplane high up in the sky. Jesus was standing on a cloud, waiting for me to walk to Him. I gathered my courage and nervously stepped out of the plane and onto the air, keeping my eyes on Him. I walked on air all the way to Jesus and took His hands. Instantly, I could feel an adjustment in my spirit as I rested in this place. All nervousness had gone, replaced by calm assurance.

By constantly using your faith, the life of

> ***Christ will be released deep inside you, and the resting place of his love will become the very source and root of your life.***
>
> **—Ephesians 3:17**

Meanwhile, our Turkish friend was definitely not interested in Christianity. Messaging led nowhere. But in my spirit, I took leaps of faith and followed the Holy Spirit the best I could. At one point, I remember writing down everything I felt Him saying, including the plans God had for this man. I thought to myself, "This can't be Jesus." Immediately, I heard Him say, "John 4:26." Curious now, I looked it up. It said, *"Then Jesus declared, 'I who speak to you am he.'"*

Astounded, and suitably chastened, I kept writing in my journal what I felt the Lord prophesying over this Muslim friend. A few sentences later, again, I doubted. I had surprised even myself, that I could doubt, having just received such an astonishing confirmation from God. I didn't even know that verse was in the Bible! But here I was. I prayed, "I'm sorry, Lord." Then out of my mouth started flowing new words in a new tongue that I hadn't spoken in before. It was comforting, soothing, and I continued speaking, not understanding any of what I was saying. This time, I didn't doubt but was filled with awe that the Lord was so gentle and kind with me—not upset with my doubt, but repeatedly showing me that He was really the One leading me in prayer.

After several months of praying for this man, I suddenly felt a quietness in my spirit and wondered, "Is it over?" By listening to my spirit, I simply knew that my time to pray for him was closing. Apparently, he was not destined to be my son-in-law, and so far, he showed no interest in Christianity. However, with thankfulness, I left him in the Father's hands. It is a mystery to me because I didn't see the fruit of my prayers. Even today, I am grateful for his friendship as well as the intensity of the Holy Spirit, my new prayer language, and how God led me to follow the Spirit in exciting adventures in prayer, which gave me an increase in faith.

I believe Jesus had invited me into this new level of faith because it propelled me into a totally new season of revelation, lasting for three years. God had wonderful plans to rescue me from my tangled soul, and it required this new level of faith to go into unknown territory: directly into the depths of my heart.

FIVE

HEART HEALING

He sent me to heal the wounds of the brokenhearted, to tell captives, "You are free," and to tell prisoners, "Be free from your darkness." to strengthen those crushed by despair who mourn in Zion—to give them a beautiful bouquet in the place of ashes, the oil of bliss instead of tears, and the mantle of joyous praise instead of the spirit of heaviness. Because of this, they will be known as Mighty Oaks of Righteousness, planted by Yahweh as a living display of his glory.

—Isaiah 61:1, 3—

"Where are your bright colors!?" Skye, one of my prayer partners shouted—at least it felt like she was shouting to my spirit. I knew exactly what she meant.

"I KNOW!!" I responded emphatically, "I feel like I'm strangled in my personality!"

This strangulation of my personality, a profound inability to let myself out, gave me a feeling of not being seen or known, not even by myself. To be free from it was my deepest heart cry. This is a story of how the Lord encountered my fears, doubts, and shame and brought me into a tangible revelation of being His beloved daughter, significant beyond measure, beautiful, adored, accepted as I am, and free to be my true self, as He created me to be. This journey has broken off my chains, and I am so excited to share this season with you. My story is for all of us in bondage, chains, and prisons, who want to be free to be themselves. The Father has already sent Jesus to unlock our freedom and destinies. He is actively working out the victory in our hearts. My revelations and victories are yours also to receive. Let's believe together!

THE EXPERIMENT

We were cozied up on the couches, that is, my sister Deanna and I, along with my friends, Skye and Sheryl, having recently begun an experiment with the Lord in praying together. I had wondered why our private prayer life was vibrant, full of God's presence, but in contrast, praying together with others was empty and boring. Why was this? We decided that it was because when we were with someone, we didn't dare to listen to the Lord's voice and speak out what we thought He was saying for fear of being wrong. Thus began the experiment. What would happen, we asked, if we spoke out everything we heard or sensed in our minds? Even if we thought we were 100% convinced it was NOT God and completely our own random thoughts? Ok, Deanna and I agreed, let's try it and see what happens. The rule would be: say everything that comes to mind.

We bowed our heads in prayer. Immediately I hear, "You are Peter and on this rock, I will build my church." Deanna looks at me with knowing eyes.

"Remember the rule!" she says. I choke out the words, already embarrassed but also in wonder. We conclude that we have no idea what it means. We might be Peter? What is the rock, and what do we have to do with God building His church? Let's ask Him.

We gather another time and see a set of keys. In awe, Deanna reads the next verse after the scripture I heard previously, and it says, "I have given you the keys to the kingdom of heaven." We gasped in amazement that this might be true, having never heard of this type of revelation where we lived in a small mountain town in British Columbia, Canada. Yet, the Holy Spirit's presence was tangible, even weighty, and proceeded to lead us on a fast-paced and exciting journey of revelation and healing that continued in the same vein for three years.

One thing I really hated was feeling embarrassed. It was awkward at best and humiliating at worst. However, I have lived without understanding how to escape it. Many things I have said or done in normal conversations with colleagues or friends have left me feeling exposed and ashamed. Looking back, I am convinced that no one ever noticed or remembered these things. This was simply my personal prison.

Nothing worked to free me from this prison in my soul and it was humiliating. I had a career I loved, I was married and in love, and I had the best children in the world. Still, my battle with feeling "less than" was raging quietly under the surface as the years went by. I longed to experience the tangible love of the Father and cried out to Him for His love. He then gave me two dreams. In the first one, I was a few feet off the ground, and

I was encouraged to be "getting there." In the second dream, I had an encounter with Jesus and experienced His indescribably accepting love under a lovely garden gazebo. It was incredible. Yet, when I woke up, I could not find it.

I continued to feel a pervading sense of shame and nothing seemed to shift it. I felt I was in prison with no freedom in my personality and a slave to the fear of what others might think about me. If someone was unfriendly to me, tears sparked in my eyes, and I had to turn the corner and hide. I was once speaking to a man in the grocery store about the price of butter, and my face went beet red over which butter to buy! Even when I would be walking with my best friend, at some point in our conversation I would feel the familiar discomfort rise up and could not explain why. I had experienced incredible things with the Lord, but my feelings of being "less than" and embarrassed over anything I might say to people intensified. I was desperate for a breakthrough of freedom to simply be myself.

MY RELEASE FROM PRISON

I tried to hang onto Skye's words, though they felt too much to even grasp: "Your freedom is not just for you; it's to free many people from demons." Wow, I had no idea what she was talking about. The next thing that happened was the most simple, yet profound, thing I had yet encountered. It was the beginning of my release from prison. Sheryl said, "I see a small dungeon room with a large wooden door, and you are there, as a very young girl, sitting on a stool. Jesus is standing at the open door, offering to take your hand. Will you take it?" I took His hand, and I still remember the wide, spacious land that we walked into. It felt so good to be out of the dungeon room! Was it this simple? Yes. I trusted the presence of the Holy Spirit along with His peace, and thanks to Father's gift of faith, doubt was not pestering me! Knowing He is leading changes everything.

> ***But it was because of our rebellious deeds that he was pierced and because of our sins that he was crushed. He endured the punishment that made us completely whole, and in his wounding we found our healing.***
>
> ***—Isaiah 53:5***

TEAM

The great thing about praying with a team of two or more people that you trust is that different people have different gifts. One person sees an image while another gets a scripture verse. Another prays in the spirit, and another receives accurate information about events, places, people, and times. Together, over time, we went from never hearing about healing prayer, to listening in the Spirit together. The Holy Spirit led us in stunning accuracy and almost everything we heard was Him.

Every time we got together, we simply sat down and prayed, "God, what do you want to do today?" Then waited. Someone would get a picture, a word, a scripture, or a sense of something for a person in the group. Oftentimes, forgiveness was required. Walls fell down. We let many things go. Many lies were exchanged for His truth. Sometimes the way through fear was walking right into the midst of it in our imagination. Each session was unique and powerful. Listening to the Spirit about where to go and what to do next was all that was required. Having our Bibles handy and a cup of tea was great as well.

HEALING PRAYER KEYS

Our prayer times were so exciting that we began praying at every opportunity in our busy family lives, which was at least once a week for 2-3 hours. We would sit down and wonder at the presence of God before we even began. Here are three keys He showed us:

1. BE VULNERABLE. Our broken places are the ones that need healing. Being completely transparent, trusting the Holy Spirit with all our defenses down, makes all the difference. Even when we aren't aware, stay open. If we knew already, we probably wouldn't still be where we are. Inviting Him in to reveal where He was in a memory, that alone can heal.
2. EXPERIMENT. Ask for everything. If we were unsure of a picture, we just asked more questions. If we felt an impulse, we tried it. Be unhinged from what you know so far. Go back into your family ancestry to discover what Father wants to reveal. Don't be afraid to speak to yourself in the womb or invite Jesus there. Ask for new strategies, and enjoy the freedom of not knowing what's next.
3. BELIEVE. Complete dependence on God alone to show us what He wants to do and how to do it boosts faith quickly. We started with nothing, but an idea and the Holy Spirit soon brought images, questions, memories, blocks, solutions, and everything required. Often, He met us in painful memories and spoke hope, truth, and healing to our hearts. When truth is revealed, all that's left is for us to believe.

You can always be sure that His will is for you to come into the confidence of knowing who He made you to be. You are most certainly more incredible than you can imagine! Loving yourself will set you free to love other people because you won't need to defend yourself or even be concerned about yourself. Your feet will come to rest on the Rock of Jesus Christ. He wants your heart and thinking to come into agreement with His.

> ***And this is the confidence that we have toward him, that if we ask anything according to his will he hears us. And if we know that he hears us in whatever we ask, we know that we have the requests that we have asked of him.***
>
> **—1 John 5:14-15**

The reward of leaving an evening of prayer feeling lighthearted, seen, understood, and loved after being open and vulnerable was amazing. One of the ways we would know if healing had come was to go back into our memory and check if there was still pain. If there was, we would continue listening to the Father, forgiving and letting go as He led.

One of my key healing times was when the Holy Spirit led me layer by layer to uncover protective shields I had placed over my heart. I simply saw them in my mind as we prayed. Then we asked Him questions, such as, "What would You like to do with the shield?" Or, "When did this shield develop?" It was always good to ask Him where He was and what He said. There was no method; we only did what felt natural. As I allowed him to take away what I no longer needed, He actually replaced whatever was removed with a new heart that He won for me on the cross. I marveled at the raw tender heart I was experiencing. I remember falling to my knees in awe as I told my 'new heart' story to friends the following day.

FREEDOM THROUGH FORGIVENESS

I cannot adequately describe the freedom that comes from forgiveness. There is an immediate lightening effect. When Jesus told us to cast our cares on Him because His yoke is easy and His burden is light, I admit I didn't understand what He meant. I thought it happened automatically by praying for things. However, to truly cast our cares upon Him, we need to let go, and the thing that prevents us from letting go of pain is unforgiveness.

Before we forgive, we must consider what it is we are forgiving. The behavior towards us is one thing, but the heart of the matter is that something has been stolen from us. It is important before forgiving someone to consider the complete cost to our lives. Looking beyond anger, what has been stolen from me? What has it cost me—past, present, and future? And what has it cost those you love? These things are all a part of forgiveness. If you haven't considered the complete cost, then you haven't yet fully forgiven. This is often why we need to forgive multiple times, as we recognize various aspects of a situation that we didn't consider previously. By letting go and forgiving someone, we are freeing ourselves. Staying in unforgiveness is like staying chained to them and the pain. Forgiving is a gift to ourselves first, and then to everyone else affected.

There may be other reasons, but wholly canceling a debt without any expectation of repayment or even an apology is much easier when we trust Jesus with our pain. We are not letting go blindly; we are giving everything into the Father's hands. We are trusting Him to be the judge and not ourselves. Judging is not our place when it comes to issues of the heart. We usually know almost nothing about another person's heart —including their past, pain, motives, and personality lens (how they view things). We have no right to judge their actions that hurt us. Our Papa understands the pain in our hearts, and His compassion is enough. He knows how to lead us into the light where we can breathe deeply and discover new life.

WHAT IS GOD LIKE?

When you imagine God the Father, what do you see? What about Jesus and the Holy Spirit? If your images are aligned with God's goodness and His love for you, then you will have an easier time trusting Him with the vulnerable parts of your life. How easy or difficult we find it to be vulnerable with God will depend on who we believe Him to be. Usually, there are many ideas of Him that He needs to expose so that we will understand what we think about Him.

As I forgave my parents for being broken themselves, as we all are, and how it has affected my life and also my children's lives, my view of God started changing. Father showed me memories that revealed where He was for me and offered me His perspective on a situation. I came to understand that He is my true Father, and there is nothing He cannot heal. I love my parents, and I can see how they are also a reflection of His character, even though I do not expect them to be perfect. They are allowed to have pain and make mistakes, just like I am. This is a beautiful place to be. I am free to live in the blessing they are to me and our entire family. With their sincere faith, they have opened the heavens and released incredible blessings over us.

My parents have gifted us with a life-giving perspective that sees possibilities instead of problems and a fierce determination to stand in love, freedom, and hospitality through all seasons of life.

One of the amazing parts of God is that He is above male and female. Both man and woman are made in His image and came from Him. Therefore, He holds the best of all male and female attributes in who He is. Likewise, we are all a combination of what we might typically call male and female characteristics. No one carries only male or only female qualities.

Female attributes often offer comfort, safety, nurturing, gentleness, and kindness—much like a soft pillow. However, the power of such comfort is stability and strength, knowing and receiving the value of our emotions. A buffer of comfort from home might ward off attempts to find comfort in illegitimate places that end up inviting more harm than good, or at least only temporary relief. The beauty of comfort from our parents is that we are better set up to receive comfort from the Holy Spirit and from the Father Himself.

Masculine attributes tend to naturally align with being a source of strength and purpose. There is an energy around male strength that may also be more evident in some females since we are uniquely created. This masculine energy is motivating and inspiring. There is a belief for the impossible and hope for greatness. We often receive from our dads the inspiration to achieve the desires of our hearts and are willing to go to great lengths for success.

As I come to understand the vastness of who the Father is for me, He becomes my safe place. Now, I tend to find myself leaning on His chest, knowing He is my comforter, my strength, and the One who never leaves me. He also inspires me to connect with my passions and achieve things of value to me. I sense the wind of the Spirit in connection with Him, and His energy runs through me. I am a daughter, and I delight in having a Father.

Experiences in these prayer times were life-changing for me, and I started to share with others a little of what God had done. I began to experience lightheartedness in my spirit, whether walking on the street, teaching, or being with my family. My children were teenagers by now, and I delighted in parenting them in a way that allowed freedom in their decision making and coaching them rather than controlling their behavior. A rising confidence allowed me to let go and allow them to make their own mistakes. Our conversations filled me with anticipation as I wondered how they would choose to live their lives. Lightheartedness began to permeate my life.

I watched insecurity evaporate as my heart began to feel free from judgment. Suddenly, I began chatting with people around town in my daily interactions. This was such new ground for me! I would ask the grocery clerk how she was doing. I would chat with the people in line about the fresh produce. Each engagement filled me with thankfulness to God and even now I am overwhelmed with gratitude. I could interact with friends and strangers without feeling embarrassed or ashamed of who I was. What other people may take for granted, I knew to be a spectacular healing of my heart. Confidence started to soar naturally in my spirit.

> ***Hold on to what you have so that no one will take your crown.***
>
> **—Revelation 3:11**

I began to receive scriptures from the Holy Spirit such as Revelation 3:11. He gave this scripture to me one morning while I was sitting in my brown corduroy chair, where I usually sat with Him in the early mornings. I curiously looked it up and it said: "***Hold on to what you have so that no one will take your crown.***" Studying further, I found that this particular crown is a crown of righteousness. I knew that this is what was won on the cross in the healing of my heart. I needed to hold tightly to it so that I wouldn't lose ground. I asked the Lord how I should do this, and He gave me the image of a sword. It was beautiful and sharp, decorated with blue stones that represented my healing.

The sword is a weapon, and we are to use it as a defense against the enemy. In Ephesians 6, the sword of the spirit is part of our armor and is called the Word of God. The Word of God is full of incredible declarations about who we are and who God is for us. Incredibly, these truths now had a place to land in my heart. My bright colors were starting to shine as His love began to take root.

> "The beauty of the Father's love in sending Jesus to earth to reveal His heart for us, is that now we are in the flow of a rich, powerful dynamic love that does not depend upon us."[1] —Dass Supperamanium

---

It was interesting to see how that affected my relationship with Brian. For one, he could see that the Father was breathing new life into me. I was happy, unaffected by his moods, and starting to consider new options in things I would love to do. I was talking about opening a coffee shop. Soon, I noticed that my husband's love for me, though always constant, was invigorated as he watched me become more alive.

LOVE IS WHAT SOFTENS HEARTS

For all of our marriage, I had been praying for Brian's heart to soften, but the Lord first healed my heart, and then He used me to soften Brian's heart. Love is what softens hearts. I had it all wrong. However, now that I wasn't dependent on Brian for my value, I could speak life into his broken places.

"I will always listen and help you," I whispered to him. We began to assume the best of each other, and Brian consistently became the man I always believed him to be: gentle, respectful, funny, strong, wise, protective, loving, and much more.

When we occasionally came into conflict, I was no longer the same person. He could see in my eyes that I meant what I said. My value had increased in my own eyes as I recognized how God had always been loving me, through all of my life. Therefore, I knew that I was worth respecting and being treated with kindness, even in conflict. Now that I knew this, somehow it was totally wrong to offer anything but love and respect to each other. Brian sensed it, too. Perhaps it was the transparency on my face going from joyful to hurt, without hiding or being defensive. Perhaps he has a whole different story of what was happening in his own heart. All I know is that my healing brought me great joy. Uncontainable joy, which I will share in the next chapter.

SIX
JOY

The fruit produced by the Holy Spirit
within you is divine love in all its varied expressions:
joy that overflows
—Galatians 5:22—

"No, you are MY joy."

Maybe this is why children skip so much. It was almost as if my feet were not touching the ground. It was like I had a magical secret inside of me, and no one really knew. It's not like I didn't tell people what God was doing, but the truth is, to how many people do you explain the details of your emotions and nuances of doubt or anxiety? There were places in my heart that felt free because of the healing and love I had received.

Joy was natural, and I no longer needed to focus on positive thinking, which was what I was used to. The difference now was that my mind was free because my heart was free. For the most part, positive thinking had worked fairly well for me in the past, propping up my emotions. But now I knew that the lies I had believed had been exchanged for the truth of God's love and who He said I was. Walls had been torn down. This changed everything!

Inside of me, I was filled with a lightness in my spirit that had me giggling with joy when no one was looking. Joy was the natural result of freedom welling up in my heart. As the walls around my heart came crashing down, I felt more of my heart flowing out towards other people.

One year, my husband and I went away for a weekend get-away before Christmas. We bought tickets for a local showing of "How the Grinch Stole Christmas." I was so excited. As we relaxed into our red velvety seats, I began noticing the faces of all the people in the theatre—details of the expressions on their faces, what they were wearing, and who they came to the play with. Some people caught my eye, and I could feel myself smile back. My heart naturally began interceding for each person, silently, from a desire to bless and release this joy I felt to everyone around. This continued through the entire play as I casually enjoyed the show with this dynamic intercession going on underneath. By the time we left the theatre, I was ecstatic. Walking hand in hand, I told my husband what I had been doing. I explained, "I'm so happy. I feel like my feet aren't touching the ground again!" I had never experienced such delight.

Staying in joy meant living with my heart wide open and aligning my perspective with where the Father was at work. As He shared His heart with me for all the people around me in the theatre, I allowed His love to pour through my prayers. It was a simple opening of my heart and doing what felt natural in my spirit. Sometimes, I have a way of suffocating my spirit with thoughts of what I "should" be doing when the perspective of heaven is a whole different track. Now I was learning a new way, and joy was my reward. I wonder about the busy lives we live and how often we might be quenching the Spirit. With COVID-19, so many of our lives have slowed down where, previously, we thought this was impossible. It will be interesting to see how many hearts are re-evaluating their priorities and enjoying the rest of a more relaxed pace of life.

HOW DO I KEEP MY JOY?

The biggest joy-stealers for me have been condemnation, fear, and doubt. While much negative clamor simply ended when the root was exposed and my heart was healed from long-standing lies around unworthiness and shame, as discussed in chapter five, my thoughts more easily lined up with what gave me life. Let's consider a few of these joy-stealers.

JOY-STEALER: CONDEMNATION

It is impossible to live under condemnation and feel joyful at the same time. Check where you might be in agreement with self-condemnation, or perhaps you are weighed down by someone else's opinion of you. Maybe we have made a mistake that we need to sincerely apologize for, make amends for, and understand their consequences in other people's lives. Perhaps this is an issue that we need to bring to the Lord for His healing and there are things He wants us to let go of and trust Him with. Friend, let's trust Him.

In any case, there is no condemnation over you in the Father's eyes. We are completely forgiven in Christ, set free, and all of our enemies have been defeated. This takes a lifetime of growing in faith and trusting the Father to lead us through victoriously, but in our position as His child, He is always proud of us, always on our side, always fighting for us, and, remarkably, He is always pronouncing us innocent.

> ***Those who look to Him are radiant, their faces are never covered in shame.***
>
> **—Psalm 34:1, NIV**

JOY-STEALER: FEAR

Anxiety reveals an idol in our hearts that we're bowing down to. My weakness is my children. If something is seriously wrong, I have to battle fear and trust that the Father really is fathering them right now. Trusting Him means I am not living in fear, and this can take some positioning on my part:

- Letting go of control
- Breaking agreement with fear
- Trusting in God's goodness
- Listening for His voice
- Believing His word
- Resting in His love
- And returning to worship

I have an emotion that I call "on high alert." It doesn't feel like fear, but it motivates me to intercede continually or act in a way that seems helpful for the situation. There is a place in the middle of a storm that is calm, which is called the eye. It's an interesting name, considering that we cannot see clearly when we are in fear. But in the eye of the storm, we see clearly. We are at peace, yet on high alert, ready, and able to respond quickly and confidently as needed.

JOY-STEALER: DOUBT

I have expressed that doubt is certainly my most difficult battle. On the other hand, faith in my life has produced extraordinary joy. A battle with faith has also seemed to precede, or stand at the gate, of every victory. Walking in faith is easy, once we have arrived. This is where we are dangerous warriors, able to defeat the enemy easily, totally dependent on God's power to win the battle. But stepping up my faith into a new level is what I find terrifying. Doubt is an enemy to keep us limited in our influence and bound up, and it certainly steals our joy. Without joy, is there really evidence of faith? We want to win this battle to believe, because joyful love overflowing from our hearts is worth fighting for. At the same time, we recognize that our part is simply to believe and rest in our Father's love as He leads us in our lives.

> ***God! Arise with awesome power, and every one of your enemies will scatter in fear! Chase them away—all these God-haters. Blow them away as a puff of smoke. Melt them away like wax in the fire. One good look at you and the wicked vanish.***
> ***But let all your godly lovers be glad! Yes, let them all rejoice in your presence and be carried away with gladness. Let them laugh and be radiant with joy!***

> ***Let them sing their celebration-songs for the coming of the cloud rider whose name is Yah!***
> ***To the fatherless he is a father. To the widow he is a champion friend. To the lonely he makes them part of a family.***
> ***To the prisoners he leads into prosperity until they sing for joy.***
> ***This is our Holy God in his Holy Place!***
>
> **—Psalm 68:1-6**

NEW NAME

I began noticing that when someone would call my name, it felt odd. How strange is that? It was like I felt uncomfortable with my own name, like a shoe that doesn't exactly fit. I asked the Lord, "Do I have a new name?!" I felt a little jump in my spirit, and so I responded, "Show me." Within a few weeks, I was listening to Beth Moore explain the Greek meaning of the word "chara." She defined it as "joy for a reason." My heart immediately burst in recognition. "I have joy for a reason!" I thought.

In a flash, my mind tried to comprehend what my spirit already recognized. The word "chara" had the accent on the second syllable (pronounced kar-ahh'), which made an already difficult word harder to pronounce. I played with the syllables and put the accent on the first syllable (car'-ah). My ladies Bible study group noticed the look on my face, and so I described what had just happened. My new friend Lara immediately commented, "You are more of a Chara than anything. It suits you perfectly." Everyone agreed. Could this really be God?

I decided to put out a fleece. I told the Lord to please confirm my name through my husband. Brian was not frivolous or flaky in any way, but conservative and practical. He was a doer and a wise man. Our relationship was now strong, and I knew he wouldn't hesitate to be honest with me. It was our Valentine's Day dinner coming up, and I thought it would be the perfect time. I explained my story. He listened silently, then he pulled out his Valentine's Day card, crossed out my old name, and wrote: Chara. He handed it gently to me with a smile. My heart overflowed.

Changing your name feels equivalent to changing your identity. This is not something I did lightly. What would my parents say? I didn't want to hurt their feelings. The old me would never, ever do anything crazy like this. She would have been too worried about what people would think—too nervous to carry it through, and it would have been a disaster. However, who I was now was elated with the idea. Father was actually changing my name? This reinforced His pleasure in me, and I responded by worshipping Him anew.

YOU ARE MY JOY

"I have joy for a reason—You are My joy," I told the Father again, remembering my past three years of transformational healing. Instantly, I felt His reply, "No, Chara, you are My joy." My mind reeled to take in what He said. I had to take a deep breath and consider what I just heard. Could it really be?! Fortunately, I was praying with my sister, so she could encourage me to accept what He said. She reminded me that He is really that good—beyond what we can comprehend! This was something that He would tell me over and over again in the years to come. One time, I was simply walking down a staircase, and I quietly but clearly heard God say again, "You are My joy." I smiled shyly to myself, continuing down the stairs, but again, I wondered in amazement how I might be my Father's joy. As my faith kept moving a little higher with the next season of my life, I gradually came to believe it, and my heart filled with awe.

I decided to formally change my name on my birthday coming up four weeks later. That gave time for the idea to percolate before I began paperwork on the legal name change process. As it happens, within that time, my friend spontaneously invited me to join her on a trip to Haiti where her daughter was on missions as a midwife. Haiti is an incredible place, full of vibrancy. I felt like I was brought back in time to the seventies, riding in the back of a pick-up truck with the wind blowing on my face. I loved the scooter cabs, weaving in and out of traffic. In the open-air market, I could find raw cacao, fresh cinnamon, star anise, and coconuts to make homemade hot chocolate and real salt, dried from the ocean.

However, the thing that struck me most about Haiti was the intense spiritual climate. Unlike North America, everyone I met was open about their spiritual life, including family demons they seemed to know by name. Christianity was mixed with voodoo, and in the sampling of open-hearted locals I encountered, it seemed to resemble a traumatic roller coaster ride involving life and death situations.

I absolutely loved it—even the pigs walking in the alley, the fresh mangoes on the trees—amazing. Not to mention hiking into the green tropical forest where we swam in lonely pools of milky blue mineral water, called Bassin Bleu. What a mix of memorable experiences, and I've only just begun!

WARFARE

In the midst of vibrant Haitian life, three days before my birthday, I began to seriously doubt this whole name change idea. Suddenly, I loved my given name. It felt comforting and solid to me—grounding. I didn't want a new name that I knew next to nothing about. That's not who I am, I thought to myself. In my mind, I began to engage in a serious battle. One side of me wanted to withdraw into the comfort of the familiar. The other part of me knew that spiritual warfare is real and likely what was happening.

The Father had given me scriptures about defending my territory and holding onto what I have so that no one will take my crown. I knew that in my heart I had received so much healing. This name change was Father's gift to me. It would be a weapon of testimony and declaration of what He had done and my true identity: I was His joy. It's all clear to me now, but at the time, this voice and these thoughts were so quiet, I could barely hear them. But I hung onto them tightly, with all I had. I mustered what courage I had, and the day my birthday arrived, I was nervous, but ready. My friends anointed me with oil and declared blessings over my name. They called me Chara and this turning point set off a whole new season of blessing and continued victory throughout the next year.

I learned to take seriously the quiet voice of the Lord. The clamoring voices of opposing thoughts may be loud, but the deafening thunder almost gives it away as a distraction from what God is doing. I noticed immediately a peace that filled my heart as soon as I was through the other side of the battle. Imagine what the Lord might do through our lives if we never abandoned ship and believed Him at every turn.

BRIDE TO JESUS

In one of our prayer times towards the end of that same year, December 12, 2012, Jesus gave me a box with a ring inside. The ring had a blue stone on it. I recognized the blue stone as being the same as the stones He had given me on my sword when He showed me to defend my new ground.

I looked at the unique ring and wondered what to do with it. Luckily, I was with my sister again, who said, as usual, "Let's ask Him." Immediately, I saw Jesus on His knees and ready to put the ring on my finger. Considering I already happily had my wedding ring on that finger, I was slightly puzzled but let Him slide the ring over the top of my wedding ring. At the time, it was not an emotional experience, but I would soon look back to this encounter as not only a sign to trust Him no matter what, but also a lifeline from my Lord, who loves me.

SEVEN
TRAGEDY

"The door that requires the most sacrifice will always take us to the highest level."[1]
—Rick Joyner—

The morning began much like any other. My husband Brian left early for work around 6:30 am as he always did, with a kiss and a quick goodbye. I was curled up in my brown corduroy "chair-and-a-half," having my quiet time with the Lord before work, as usual.

Brian and I had spent the long weekend in February at home instead of having a weekend away in Spokane, as originally planned. We went out for an early Valentine's dinner and then soaked in the cave and pools at Ainsworth hot springs. We were feeling particularly close to each other because, after twenty-three and a half years of marriage, we finally had a breakthrough in our communication.

For the first time in our marriage, he listened to what was on my heart, which had the immediate effect of making me feel so loved. I knew we were in a brand new place when I said I wanted to talk that Saturday afternoon, and, instead of storming out the bedroom door defensively, he not only listened, but also heard what was on my heart. Mutually responding with warmth and understanding was totally new ground for us. The depth of intimacy that happened between us that night burst out in silent tears streaming down my face as Brian held me. Our hearts were finally connected.

Yes, it had been tough over the years, to say the least. It felt like a slow, steady battle, almost like a war zone, with periods of peacetime negotiations. Periodically, we would gain ground by being transparent with one another. Family life was amazingly peaceful and much fun, but the battle for our marriage had been about having an intimate heart connection with deep authenticity. Thankfully now, with the kids graduating high school, I looked warmly at Brian and knew that our marriage had actually made it through the fire. Exciting plans for the years ahead were in the works, spending six months together in Turkey and spying out ideas for retirement.

> ***Everything I've taught you is so that the peace which is in me will be in you and will give you great confidence as you rest in me. For in this unbelieving world you will experience trouble and sorrows, but you must be courageous, for I have conquered the world!***
>
> **—John 16:33**

The phone call came after the long weekend on Tuesday, February 12th, 2013, at 8:30 am. I was at work wearing pajamas for Pajama Day, and students were arriving, fluttering about in childish excitement. Years later, I was again the principal and now a junior high teacher at the small private Christian school where I had invested much of my heart. It was my son, Brett:

> Mom, you should come now to Dad's school.
>
> Why?
>
> He's not doing well.
>
> What's happening?
>
> He's having trouble breathing.
>
> Breathing?
>
> Ya.
>
> What do you mean? That doesn't make sense.
>
> He's unconscious, and they're doing CPR on him—maybe come right to the hospital.

Instantly, I was on full alert. Briefly, I told my secretary and friend that my husband was unconscious, jumped in my Rav4, and immediately started praying. Hands firmly on the steering wheel, I called Brian to life, to healing, to experience the love of God, for angels to minister to him, and for him to encounter God, "right now," in fullness.

The presence of God filled the vehicle, and my mind was crystal clear. I was completely calm, winding along the curvy road with the rush hour traffic at a steady speed of 80km/hour to Castlegar where Brian taught elementary school. Because the presence of the Holy Spirit was so strong, I was totally confident that my prayers were not only heard, but answered. I continued praying full force the whole way, uninterrupted and believing he would be okay.

I parked unhurriedly, walked to the front desk, and asked to see Brian Rigby, my husband. The nurse looked surprised and hesitant, so I repeated myself. She led me into the small waiting room where my son was waiting, and we embraced emotionally. I vaguely noticed another man there, too, a teacher who had performed CPR on Brian when he collapsed. I took in the distress on Brett's face and the tears rolling down his cheeks.

Brian had called Brett at home to take him to the hospital. I guess he was having trouble breathing and then collapsed in a heart attack. But walking into the hospital now, in the presence of God, full of peace and confidence, I encouraged my son with words of faith, speaking life and hope into his shoulder as we held each other.

Soon, a doctor walked in, sat down, and briefly explained that they had performed CPR on my husband for close to an hour, but unfortunately, he did not make it.

"WHAT?!! Those are the wrong words!" I exclaimed. My mind reeled to take in what she was saying. I needed to see him for myself.

I spent the next 5 hours or so with Brian, soaking in this last opportunity to be with him. The door was closed, and we were alone in a stark hospital supply room—Brett, myself, and Brian's body on a stretcher. Remarkably, the peace of God filled the space. I yanked the tube out of my husband's mouth because it was distorting his face. His expression was relaxed and peaceful, with a hint of a smile. I asked the nurse for supplies to bathe his body, longing for any meaningful last connection. At one point, even laying my body on top of his, I absorbed the lingering heat still remaining and felt how his body contour fit into mine, soaking in this familiar comfort for the final time. *Do you feel God's presence here?* I asked the hospital staff when they popped in. *Yes, It's very peaceful in here,* they'd respond.

At one point, a nurse knocked on the door to tell me my Uncle Jim was here. I don't know anyone named Jim, I answered, and closed the door. Then it dawned on me—how could I not know Jim! We are actually very close. I went to meet him and Pastor Jesse. After hugs and tears, I said, Come see Brian! I wanted to stay in his room and share the peace there with others. For most of the day, Brett and I spoke openly to Brian, we took turns being alone with him and were in no hurry to go home.

On the way home from the hospital, I told my son that I really felt that those were exactly the number of Dad's days that he had to live on earth. I had an inner assurance that if God knew this would happen from the beginning, then He must have a plan for us to get through. Brett had felt the same thing amidst our shock, grief, and sadness. We took comfort in knowing that God was aware of how long Brian's life would be. And now, Brian was still alive in heaven. I spent time imagining him there and what he might be doing.

My immediate response was thankfulness that I was chosen to be part of Brian's life. I knew our journey had been a wild ride, complete with excitement, difficult challenges, and adventures. We had grown so much and raised a family together that we loved. Brian and I knew each other like no one else, and the trust we had built over the decades was unshakeable—somehow I was especially thankful for trust. Through our worst times, we managed to love each other, and Brian was a rock like no other. I was bursting with thankfulness for all we had come through.

For two decades my heart had cried for the intimate connection that we finally discovered. I also knew that for my part in fighting for our marriage, the Father was proud of me. I don't know exactly how I knew this, except that I felt His pleasure in me. It wasn't that I did it all right, but I persevered, depended on Him, and to my wonder, our marriage survived the fire, stronger than ever. I have no doubt that the Father was telling Brian how proud He was of him as well. I knew that right in this moment, Brian was still loving me from heaven, with purity and insight he never had before.

I like to believe he can pray for us from heaven and that the Father gives him updates. Thankfulness exploded in me for this, and also for the relational nearness that was especially evident in detailed events of the week before he died, both with me and our two children. God had even sent a snowstorm when Brian drove my daughter Jenna to the airport a few days before he died, and they were compelled to spend a cozy night in a hotel room, just the 2 of them for the first time ever. Furthermore, Brian sent a beautiful text of encouragement to her the morning he died, expressing how proud he was of her, as she was investigating colleges in Ontario. How amazing it feels for someone's love to strengthen us, even in death!

> ***Living within you is the Christ who floods you with the expectation of glory! This***

> ***mystery of Christ, embedded within us, becomes a heavenly treasure chest of hope filled with the riches of glory for his people, and God wants everyone to know it!***
>
> **—Colossians 1:27**

I STILL HAVE GOOD PLANS FOR YOUR LIFE

I was trembling as I stood staring at our queen bed that first night. My sister Karen sat me on the mattress, praying over me, as I battled with going to sleep without my husband. Thankfully, Karen stayed with me. In the morning, she asked me how I slept.

"STILL," I mumbled. "In the night, God said that He STILL has good plans for my life." Actually, I had slept through the night and remembered this one dream. I was shocked. Somehow, I had already assumed my life was over. This promise kept my eyes focused on God's plans for me and brought me great hope. Karen gave me a heart necklace that was engraved, 'STILL' on the back. I hung onto God's promise that He still had good plans for me with all my might.

> ***For our spiritual wealth is in him, like hidden treasure waiting to be discovered.***
>
> **—Colossians 2:3**

One thing I noticed about grief is that multiple emotions seemed to exist in my heart at the same time, or perhaps they freely flow from one feeling to another in just a matter of seconds. At times, the pain in my heart threatened to overwhelm me. Here I was, experiencing my worst fear. Instinctively, my eyes were laser-focused on Jesus, knowing He knew how to lead me through my tragedy. So far, He had welled up in my heart almost instant acceptance that those were the number of Brian's days, thankfulness that I was a part of his life, and the promise that He STILL had good plans for my life.

IN THE MOMENT

However, while swimming in fear of being consumed by sadness, I soon discovered a startling secret that kept me from falling off the edge: in my present moment, I seem to be okay. That was a shocking revelation the first time I discovered it! In one sense, I felt buffered by God's comforting presence, but, on the other hand, that didn't stop the pain that threatened to overwhelm me. So it stunned me when I recognized, "I'm alive... I'm breathing... In this second, in this PRESENT second, I'm not overcome!" I decided I was staying here. I had snapped a picture of a moment in time, and, in spite of my tragedy, I realized that if I could capture the present, I was better than I imagined. Let me explore this a bit further.

This revelation of living in the moment was a lifeline for me. I realized that looking back, even for a second, was too painful. Also, looking ahead to "this evening," or "tomorrow" was scary. But, at this exact moment, astonishingly, I seemed to be okay. I recognized there was a special grace to stay in the moment I was in.

In my life, I had been inspired to try to live in the moment, like this, living life in constant awareness of Jesus being with me, but with almost no success. Usually, I tended to either live in the past by mulling over regrets and torture myself over what had already happened or live in anticipation of what was to come, whether it was dinner this evening or travel plans. Yet now, the pain kept me living in the current moment, where I was constantly in the presence of God.

IN UNION WITH CHRIST

One thing was clear beyond a shadow of a doubt: Jesus knew how to walk me through this tragedy. With a heart falling to pieces, a stomach ache, and this feeling of being lost in how to even proceed through my day, I trusted Jesus to show me the way. I discovered that in this season, living in union with Jesus had a built-in buffer because if I became distracted and lost sight of Him, I immediately began to fall into despair. This brought me right back into the safety of His presence.

The Father taught me a secret that I will forever hold dear: He anoints our true self that He created us to be—the one that is real, honest, vulnerable, child-like, trusting, and dependent on Him—and as I mentioned, He communicates to our real self in our current, present moment. I normally enjoy living in my plans for the future, especially travel adventures, but all that changed in this season. I hung onto His promise that He *still* had good plans for my life, but I didn't need to know what those plans might be. There was hope in the uncertainty because my hope was Jesus. He knew where we were heading, so I resolved to rely on Him and protected that space.

In a myriad of ways, I knew Jesus was leading me through my pain, and as He led me along, I realized I was not afraid. This released so much freedom, looking at it in retrospect, to "stay in my lane." My season was one of mourning, living in the pain of my heart with the Holy Spirit, and that was enough for me at this time. I was comforted by knowing that grieving was a beautiful way to honor my husband in my heart.

TIMELESSNESS

I wonder if the reason I found relief in living in the present moment is because this is where we touch the heavenly reality of timelessness. We can only experience the Holy Spirit right now, and we can only hear from God right now. We know this when we pray and worship. Our worship connects us to His heart in this instant. He anoints our lives as we live them out. Joy is a present emotion. Every emotion is present tense, however, many of them are based on past or future events. Getting in touch with how I was feeling in the moment gave freedom for many emotions to pass through my heart.

It is amazing to think we are one with Christ. The fruits of the Spirit are Him living through us as we align with Him: love, joy, peace, patience, goodness, kindness, faithfulness, and self-control. They flow automatically through our lives as we live in the Father's love. Perhaps what I understood as living in the moment was actually timelessness that I touched in my spirit, and that is why I experienced such freedom. Selah.

Living in the moment was an unprecedented blessing which continued uninterrupted for about six weeks. After that time, I began to look just a little back and a little ahead. Seven years later, I am amazed at how much of my life I am still able to live in the moment, finding beauty in quiet and ordinary living. Uncommon peace abides in the present moment, and I thank God for this treasure.

> ***Christ's resurrection is your resurrection too.***
>
> **—Colossians 3:1**

I learned that as I journeyed with Christ through grief, pain was not something that needed to last forever, not even deep pain. The shortest pathway to whatever was next for me was right through the middle of my sorrow. Yet, by living in the present moment, you may also be surprised to discover it's easier than you imagine to embrace the journey. There is an ebb and a flow that creates an individual rhythm and time frame, perfect for who we are. Our expression of honor and love for people is a beautiful journey. With this lens, I could embrace my emotions, give space and time for releasing them, and allow myself a new normal of moving through life with the freedom to mourn within the rhythm of my day.

FREEDOM TO MOURN

I remember one day I was teaching my class shortly after Brian's death, and I managed to make it to three o'clock in the afternoon without crying. When the students left, I immediately connected with the Holy Spirit crying out, "Lord!!" and tears freely flowed as I quietly prepared my classroom for the next day. My heart missed Brian.

An hour later, I had a board meeting that I will never forget. Before leaving early, with everyone sitting around the table, I gave the principal's report while speaking in a normal voice and attending to the topics with tears flowing down my cheeks the whole time. They just wouldn't be contained any longer. I saw the gentleness in each board member's eyes and the appreciation they felt for my pain as we were discussing practical agenda items. This is such a glorious picture of freedom for me, being able to live my life authentically and trusting in the compassion of people.

I had spent years fearing the death of first, my dad, and then, my husband, terrified that I wouldn't be strong enough to handle it. When Brian died, I was surprised to find that pain was not the worst thing—the worst thing was depression, stemming from hopelessness. I experienced this after waking up a couple of mornings in a row feeling heavy, discouraged, and not wanting to get out of bed. I asked myself what was going on, and immediately I realized that I had slipped into self-pity. I had thoughts like, "Our kids were leaving home in the fall, and we were to begin a whole new chapter! We had fought so hard for intimacy, and now this!?"

It seemed totally unfair that after battling for two decades for our marriage, and finally flowing in peace, trust, and openhearted love in the past year especially, that Brian should die. Death felt so unnatural, so wrong! This is not how I imagined the "circle of life" to be. Well, two days of feeling sorry for myself led me straight towards depression, where I didn't feel the comforting presence of the Holy Spirit.

SELF-PITY

What are your thoughts on self-pity? What is wrong with it, and what is the line between healthy sorrow and feeling sorry for ourselves? As I remember how Jesus was leading me, I realize it was something I had to intuit with my gut. For me, several things were apparent. First of all, I suddenly felt no unity with God in that short time. This was terrifying! Perhaps it happened gradually, and I moved from living in my present moment to lamenting. However, intuitively I knew that aligning with "poor me'" was not what God's thoughts were.

Self-pity has an edge to it that we instinctively know is wrong, and we need to be honest with ourselves. If I complained about missing Brian, telling God everything I wished for, I felt His compassion. I was strengthened by hope, peace, and expectation for the good plans He still had for my life. But self-pity is the opposite of hope; it aligns with discouragement, hopelessness, rejection, fear, and doubt.

Secondly, self-pity partners with victimization. Feeling like a victim puts us in a helpless state where we are easily overcome. This is a lie. Jesus has overcome all darkness and the effects of darkness on our lives. There is victory in Him, and He is leading us in this direction where we are invited to go with Him. I refused to partner intentionally with darkness of any kind. Opening our eyes to the pit of self-pity will save us from much powerlessness.

Last of all is the false idol of self-comfort. I will admit that dwelling in self-pity is tempting, especially in letting go of dreams and the list of treasures that we had together. I fell into it without even recognizing what happened. If it wasn't for the change in my heart to sudden depression, I might still be there today! When we worship God, He alone is our comforter. When we worship ourselves, we find ways to comfort ourselves, apart from Him. One way I learned to discern if my source of comfort is from myself or from God is by either checking the fruit of how it was working overall for me or by lining it up with the way I knew Jesus to think and act.

Well, as soon as I recognized my self-pity, I remembered the black widow.

Several days after Brian died, I realized with horror that I was a widow. Aghast, I vehemently declared to myself, "I WILL NOT BE A BLACK WIDOW!" This determination was actually an expression of faith in God to lead me through this time without shame. Like my friend, Abby, has often said, "God, I will walk through the fire, but it's Your job to make sure I don't come out of it smelling like smoke!" I resolved right then, with unusual clarity, not to step into feeling sorry for myself.

It can feel impossible to switch from self-comfort, such as self-pity, to living in the true comfort of the presence of God. What helped me was having no other lifeline—that is, no other helpful options. I certainly wasn't going to rely on pamphlets on grief when God is very near to us. He is living right inside of us. Believing in Him and His ability to get you through is all you need. His love will never fail you, and He will never let you down.

Self-pity tends to move you towards giving up hope, and being thankful is suddenly impossible. It helped my perspective to realize that since the beginning of time, people had suffered death, and much worse, all around the world. The determination not to be a black widow had inadvertently saved me from self-pity and ultimately, depression. As soon as I recognized the black spider's ugly head, the light bulb turned on, and I immediately let go of self-pity and returned to thankfulness and living in the moment.

LISTENING TO MY HEART

Are you wondering about transparency with my emotions? Every day, of course, I still wanted my husband to be alive. Usually quiet by nature, I remember hollering at God in the privacy of my car, "THIS IS NOT WHAT I WANTED!! THIS IS NOT WHAT I WANTED!!" My heart exploded with complaining and sadness. I shouted and fully expressed my sorrow to Him, safely releasing my pain and resistance to Brian's death in the privacy of my vehicle. However, I never felt anger towards God. Maybe I was ticked off at the situation, but it didn't occur to me that God had made a bad decision. How could He? I trusted Him completely. He knows more than I. He knew the number of Brian's days from the beginning, and I trusted that God's purposes were accomplished for his life. The goodness of God was never in question, no matter how much I didn't like my situation.

Only three weeks had gone by, and I found myself in Cambodia on a previously arranged missions trip. My 19 year-old son, Brett, and 17 year-old daughter, Jenna, came as well. We traveled by bus to a green, rural, forested area where families lived in huts held up by poles, high off the ground. Chickens ran freely, pecking on freshly harvested rice drying on red blankets in the sunshine. We even came across a man stirring sugar palm syrup gathered from a nearby Palm tree. Golden liquid sweetness was boiling in a large copper pot over a small fire. Generously, he shared delicious chunks of palm sugar with us, which tasted a bit like maple syrup candy. We played games with the children, prayed for sick people in their homes, and were blessed by the beauty and simplicity in their daily lives.

Now, one of the days was a training day for rural pastors in Cambodia. Each of them and their wives had the opportunity to receive prayer from our team at the end of the day. It was a wonderful experience listening to the Holy Spirit and blessing them with what we were hearing from the heart of our Father. Even with little to no language communication, I sensed God moving powerfully in their hearts and in our spirits. We experienced compassion and unity in our hearts, and we loved these people. It was definitely my favorite day of the whole trip. This opened my heart even wider, if possible, than usual.

Afterward, we were all gathered together as a group for chicken soup, laughing at the chicken heads with beaks in our bowls, and sharing about our day. Meanwhile, my heart started overflowing with sadness, as I missed Brian. I don't know if it was because I was living new experiences without him, or my heart had opened wider in transparency. Tears were silently falling down my cheeks for a couple of hours while the group went through the evening.

Finally, as we were walking back to our hotel, my son put his arm around my shoulders so I could lean my head on him as we walked. We walked up a curved staircase to the second level of rooms of our heritage-style hotel. As we approached the top, I collapsed in Brett's arms, sobbing. No, not sobbing, but rather WAILING loudly from deep within, the way you would see in the old movies when a lover has died. I knew it was dramatic, but genuine grief is like that.

What anyone thought of me was not on my radar the way it always had been in the past. Going to a private place was also the last thing I cared about. Receiving comfort from the arms of my son and from the release of wailing was all I needed at that moment. I could feel the safety of Father's arms through Brett. Now, I sometimes wonder about the reaction of the people who walked by, but I am mostly grateful that they honored my need to spend a few minutes in raw grief. I am sure it was a sacrifice of peace and quiet, and I am very thankful.

THE COST

In the process of living in the moment, I had to let go of my dreams and plans for the future and rest in the hope of what God still had in store for me. There is a cost to letting go. The dearer we hold our dreams, the harder it will be to let go. This seemed to slowly happen over time. In this case, pain was my friend because it helped me to simply stay in the place where God was, in the moment, and be consumed by His presence. And that place was not in the past, where my dreams were. I found that letting go was worth everything because in the present moments I found peace, fullness, and strength.

When Brian went to heaven, I terribly missed certain things, and I didn't know what to do about it. I think there is power in naming them specifically with total honesty. I needed to acknowledge that these were real and significant losses before I could release them and accept whatever God had for me. In my journal one day, I was writing about how faith can move mountains, and if that is true, then I had some solid mountains that I needed moving. Here is my list from the spring of 2013:

- grief for what could have been
- arms not holding me at night
- love not being here for me every day
- companionship, especially on weekends and holidays
- someone to talk to about my concerns, hopes, and plans
- solid, wise advice
- having someone who accepted me as I am and allowed me to grow in freedom
- trust, won only by trials and joys of many years
- unshakeable dependability
- traditions, now forever changed
- the safety of conservative guidance
- many chores being done for me
- a proper, whole family
- having no one to love

I continued with this passionate prayer from my private journal:

> *If faith can move mountains, I say to these mountains, MOVE, in Jesus name. Let a fresh, open space come. Let not a burden of grief be on my shoulders. No! Only a joy of grief, thankful for what was and expectant for what will be. Lord, fill me anew with Your Presence. Let HOPE and LOVE flow through me, bringing refreshing and causing me to be refreshed as I bring refreshing for others.*

> ***Our own completeness is now found in him. We are completely filled with God as Christ's fullness overflows within us.***
>
> **—Colossians 2:10**

These are massive treasures that I let go of, but the trade with God is never fair—He delights in upgrading us beyond our wildest dreams! There is something spectacular that happens when God moves through us in our weak places. I had nothing to offer but my dependence on Him. It takes something big to move our independent self—who we think we "should" be—aside and simply come to Him with our open hearts.

Holy Spirit would sometimes also bring refreshing for other people through me, which totally filled me with delight. I remember saying to family members in the first week of Brian passing, "Just wait until you get here. There is peace here."

Where did it come from? Clearly it was God's peace, but how do we access it? Honestly, it was simply a by-product of intimacy with Him. Continual communication, eyes on Jesus, listening intently to my heart—these were what I could focus on.

PROTECTION

His Presence assured me of His love and protection for me. Protection means a different thing to me now than before my husband died. Life will have trouble; we know this, but through it all, there is a place of safety for my heart, which is in union with Jesus, tucked safely in God's heart. Keeping in step with the Spirit and following His lead in my heart was my emotional safety, and as it turns out, my shield—not from pain, but certainly from fear.

His compassion strengthens me. *Death, where is your sting?* On the cross, discouragement and depression were defeated. Independence was conquered. In Christ, we are brought back into the relationship with the Father that He always intended us to have. I can be completely weak, totally transparent, and dependent on Him. If I refuse to partner with discouragement, then my thoughts are focused on being in alignment with God's thoughts. These always bring life, even in death. I notice that when Jesus is leading me, the way through the dark is with our eyes on Him, connected in complete transparency.

EIGHT
SURFACING

"God, you're such a safe and
powerful place to find refuge!
You're a proven help in time of trouble—
more than enough and always available
whenever I need you."
—*Psalm 46:1*—

DREAMS

With my eyes laser-focused on Jesus and the Holy Spirit's presence constantly filling me, following my heart with childlike trust took on a whole new meaning. Without realizing it, I came to Him more as a little girl, and as I did, He showed me more about who I was.

If you're like me, you love to engage with heaven through dreams or hear stories of heaven. Several times, I experienced my husband coming to me through dreams. This always encouraged me because the reality of heaven increased for me. I saw Brian, easily recognizable, but so much more at peace, totally relaxed, unhurried, and when he left each time, he did so with such assurance that I felt strengthened. One time, I laughed because he had let his hair grow on top a bit, soft and curly, but while here, he was diligent with his every-4-week trims.

My dreams also served to show me aspects of my heart. For example, in one dream, friends were over and asking where Brian went. I answered with wonder, "I don't know! I didn't ask him!" In my dream, I'm expecting that he will return, and I will grow old with him, however, we should talk soon and work things out. Then he appeared in a white doorway, with a cheerful, "Hello!"

"Hi, Brian!" I respond, happy to see him. I saw him leaning against the doorpost, beaming with light and relaxation, confidence, and love, more than I'd ever seen. It was so comforting. The doorway often symbolizes a transition place in dreams between heaven and earth, and when I went there to ask him where he had been, he had already gone. The truth is that I don't know why he had to leave, however, I still trust God with that question rather than grieve myself with something I'll have no answer for. More importantly, I love that the dream showed that I have nothing but trust regarding my husband and am in awe of who he is in his true self in heaven.

HEAVEN

Heaven was my decorating theme for my new condo in town. Happily, I used my favorite ideas: a gorgeous coral pink wall with white satin curtains on the sliding glass doors leading to the expansive deck with a view of the blue lake and mountains, and a dark charcoal grey was painted on another wall for contrast. In the kitchen were bright yellow tiles and a massive black quartz island. Fresh white went everywhere else. An emerald green ceiling in my bedroom enveloped me in beauty in the morning, afternoon, and evening. A fireplace was surrounded with brown comfy furniture. I absolutely loved my little sanctuary.

One afternoon, I asked God if Brian had seen my new condo. Then I dozed off on the couch and entered into a dream. Brian and I were chatting casually and suddenly, in my dream, I thought—"Brian! He's here from heaven!" He then kissed me in a personal way (our secret), and as he was walking out, steadily moving towards the door, my heart was breaking as my arms were reaching after him.

"Bye!....Bye!..." I cried out. I felt like I was half awake, watching him leave. His body didn't seem solid but lighter and somehow different. I was stunned. Was Brian here?

WILL I BE HAPPY?

My heart wept, and I asked God, "Will I be happy?" I really wanted to know. Deep down inside, I had a longing for reassurance and the Father's perspective. Somehow, I knew that if there was light at the end of the tunnel, then I could give myself fully to mourning without fear of being consumed by it forever. I felt God answer me in a clear thought:

"Marriage isn't what makes someone happy.
Love makes a person happy."

This fresh revelation hit me and flowed through my mind like honey. At once I was relieved but filled with questions. Is this true? What is He saying? What love is the Father talking about? How can I access it? Is His presence His love? But I don't feel very happy!

Then, in a vision, Jesus took me by the hand, and I saw us walking and dancing on the water in my imagination. This felt comfortable and safe. Suddenly, we went IN the water!

Often, water represents the Holy Spirit—the presence and love of the Father, and we come to Him in union with Jesus. Here in the water, I abandoned myself to Him, without hesitation or reservation. Complete trust. I felt a strong, comforting presence of God all evening as I always did in this time, but this evening, He drew me into His love in a deeper way.

Whatever gave me life, that's how I sensed Jesus leading me. Crying and wailing can feel so right and good. It felt like a beautiful way to honor my husband and the natural rhythm of my heart. Laughter came easily, too. I also received love through the kindness of people.

Kindness is such a powerful force, and people's little interactions helped me so much. My hairdresser, Kyra, actually opened her salon on her day off just to fit me in for a haircut. I'm so thankful for her kindness. People brought food, treats, and flowers. I felt connected to people through eye contact, a gentle word of encouragement, and time spent with me in this season. Life was breathed into me daily in these small connections, both with friends and strangers.

Living from my heart with this much transparency felt like a completely new experience. A child is honest with their desires, dependent on their parents to lead them. With my walls down, part of letting Jesus take the wheel was doing whatever my heart wanted to do, just going there and doing that. Listening to a song, painting a picture, crying, laughing, working, daydreaming... Jesus and I were one, and I knew He was leading me through grief in the best possible way for my heart.

I remember my sister, Karen, saying to me one time, "You're becoming more yourself, the way you were when you were younger." I knew I was doing the things I wanted to do more than I could ever remember. There is freedom here. I do believe it's important to make the most of every opportunity, especially in trials, which are hard enough.

At the same time, I felt like I had a sign stamped on my forehead saying, "My husband died." Tears might pour down my face in daily transactions such as talking to a bank teller or being late for an appointment. I would explain to people, "I'm sorry, it's not you. It's that my husband died." I laugh now, but being open and honest felt right for me and saved me from trying to cover up my emotions. I was surprised how lighthearted I actually felt and how natural it was to still smile and be myself.

I noticed that strangers started smiling at me often when I walked down the street. People were exceptionally kind overall. I believe there's something about vulnerability that brings out the kindness in others. There is an openness in our eyes or face that people can see or sense, and somehow, this transparency has lasted, at least in part, until now.

I think that going through grief has changed me forever. My heart became larger and more alive, and for that, I will be forever grateful.

The secret things belong to the Lord our God, but the things that are revealed belong to us and our children forever.

—Deuteronomy 29:29, NIV

SURPRISES

When I followed the leading of my heart, it had the added benefit of discovering what makes my heart sing. Looking at the positive, such as being able to paint my walls pink or eating when I wanted to, I discovered these small things gave insight into who I am and how I wanted to live my life.

One of the significant changes in my thinking happened while out on the "Artwalk" looking at local artist creations with some friends. One painting in particular almost took my breath away. It was called "Surfacing." The blue and green colors swept me into the water where I could float, just "be," rest, and see with new eyes. Luckily, a wonderful friend said, "That's $1 per day for 10 years of looking at it. Is it worth $1 a day?" I chatted with the Lord about it. The price was way over my head. The Father asked me what I saw, and I told Him, "Water, colorful surprises, beauty, refreshing joy, and lightness in spirit." He said, "This kind of freedom is costly. It is My gift to you." This huge change in my thinking gave me freedom in my spirit that lasts until today, regardless of my financial situation.

Surprised by Joy is the title of a book written by C.S. Lewis. God surprised me, too, with joy occasionally. This was an incredible gift—simply a feeling of joy bubbling through my heart in between all my other feelings. The first time was within a few weeks of my journey. It would last a few moments but long enough for me to ponder with incredulity how one could experience joy while mourning. What wonderful assurance it was that God was with me, and it encouraged me even further to stay in unity with Him.

Thankfully, I had been living in the moment for months; otherwise, I would have been dreading the arrival of September. Both of my children set off for college and ministry school that fall. I was excited for their opportunities to begin new adventures in their lives. I wasn't too sure how I would manage myself alone though. Fortunately, in His kindness, the Lord had planned ahead and sent beautiful Liz, 14 years old and a former student that had stayed with us before, to come live with me until Christmas. She was the perfect company for me, so easy to be around, amiable, and fun. We even got a soft, beautiful puppy, Simba, who made us laugh, and Liz helped me to care for her.

When Liz left four months later, instead of being afraid of being alone, a miracle had happened in my heart. Now, each day after work, I couldn't wait to get home so I could worship and enjoy the presence of Holy Spirit. A new confidence had arisen. I loved my intimate time with God. My eyes were steadfastly on Jesus, and His presence was constantly comforting me and leading me.

This was a great key. It turns out that, as I heard spoken by Helene King, loneliness has nothing to do with being alone, but it is an issue of being disconnected from our own hearts. As I grew in my relationship with Jesus, I became fully dependent on Him for comfort, acceptance, peace, hope, and more. Loneliness eventually wasn't an issue anymore. I cannot say how it left, but I do know that it was nothing intentional I did on my part. He did it all.

Little did I understand that in loving Jesus, He was leading me to connect with my own heart. I'm guessing there's no better way than through being connected to Him. Being in Christ Jesus means we are already in the flow of love from our Father. In His eyes, we see our reflection. In His love, we know our value. To be seen by the Father is also to be validated by Him. His heart is wide open to us. Real abundant life flows from His heart to ours.

Somewhere in the stream of this daily interaction, I realized that I enjoyed my own company. I wasn't trying to make anything happen. I worshiped. I laughed at my puppy. This season was really one of letting go. I didn't have the energy to do anything except what was before me at the moment and observe with wonder the road Jesus was walking with me on. Letting go of control was the key.

God is always goodness and love. However, tragedy can reveal an idol hidden in our heart of something we are putting ahead of God. In my case, I had a couple that were sanded into dust at the same time. One was my future hopes, dreams, and plans—this idol tumbled and crashed, leaving a wide open landscape. I had drawn life from these dreams since they were exciting to think about, as Brian and I were looking forward to the options lying ahead of us. However, my dreams fell to ashes in my need to stay in the stream of what God was doing. I needed to let them all go. For some, I imagine this would be a process. Maybe it was harder than I realized for me, too; however, I was desperate to limit pain, and trusting God with my future felt fairly easy in comparison to drowning in my old hopes. Anyways, normally, I am highly flexible and enjoy new plans and adapting to new situations.

The tough one for me was the other idol that had competed for attention with God: romance. I love romantic movies and believe love is for everyone. I counted how many relationships I'd had before marriage, and it was 13! I had fallen in love each time and loved falling in love! I have a t-shirt that says: In love with love... Our marriage began and ended in a heart-warming love story that I had given everything for. And it was worth all I had. In this grieving process, I could no longer draw life from being loved by Brian, although feeling loved by him from heaven still encouraged me. Jesus was my everything—my source, my life, my love. I can still say, "I'm in love with love," but God's love is the first priority in my heart. Yes, this was strongly tested! But that is a later story.

> ***So when that day comes, you will know that I am living in the Father and that you are one with me, for I will be living in you.***
>
> **—John 14:20**

I didn't try to be one with Christ during this mourning season, but I simply was. I counted on Him to lead me. I let the Holy Spirit comfort me with His presence. Here are a few keys to peace that He showed me:

- thankfulness
- living in the present moment
- letting my heart lead me
- avoiding self-pity at all costs
- being transparent with my emotions
- being vulnerable with other people
- trusting God
- accepting my husband's death

- receiving love and life from a heavenly perspective
- doing activities that brought life
- worship

> ***Can you not discern this new day of destiny breaking forth around you? The early signs of my purposes and plans are bursting forth. The budding vines of new life are now blooming everywhere. The fragrance of their flowers whispers, "There is change in the air." Arise, my love, my beautiful companion, and run with me to the higher place. For now is the time to arise and come away with me.***
>
> **—Song of Songs 2:13**

A year and a half later, I sensed a clear shift in my spirit. To my surprise, the weighty, tangible presence of the Holy Spirit was somehow gone. I had thought He would now be with me forever. Well, I was right about that! But feeling the comforting weight of Holy Spirit continuously wasn't there anymore. I asked myself with wonder, "Is my mourning season over?" I would still feel sad now and again, but I recognized that a bright new season had begun. I felt extraordinarily thankful for how Jesus had led me right through the storm. I knew He was still with me. However, the winds had changed, and I was ready to move along. I had quit my job and was setting off for new adventures, feeling again like a 20-year-old with the world wide open to me.

Since then, the Holy Spirit continues to draw me further into the heart of the Father than I have ever gone before. In the seven years since Brian died, He has brought me from resting in the comforting presence of the Holy Spirit to experiencing depths of love with Jesus and finally, the Father. I know that all of the seasons of knowing God's love have exceeded the love I've felt in relationships with people.

The love of God is enough, in itself, to make our heart's happy. Single or married, divorced or widowed, there is a place in the heart of God where our hearts are one with His, and He is the One who invites us there. Everyone is invited. Opening our hearts to Him in faith is our part, as He knows how to clear away our barriers and restore our brokenness.

> ***Whoever passionately loves me will be passionately loved by my Father. And I will passionately love you in return and will manifest my life within you.***
>
> **—John 14:21**

PRAYING TOGETHER WITH YOU

Listen to the quiet whisper of His voice as you pray. Quiet impressions and pictures in your mind are His way of communicating with you. A thought will come from Him that may sound like your own thoughts, but better. Trust Him to speak and simply relax your mind the best you can. In Christ, you are set free, as Isaiah prophesied:

> ***The Spirit of the Lord is upon me, and he has anointed me to be hope for the poor, freedom***

> ***for the brokenhearted, and new eyes for the blind, and to preach to prisoners, 'You are set free!'***
>
> **—Luke 4:18-19**

Where is God for you right now? The Bible promises that you are in Jesus. Jesus has you with Him in the heart of the Father. They have made Their home in you. Do you have a safe place to rest in Him? Take a few moments to quiet yourself in His love. Perhaps you'd like to take time to allow your emotions to surface in your heart.

God says, "I *STILL* have good plans for your life." Will you trust Him? Are you ready to let go of the unknown? He will help you surrender the plans that you envisioned. Will you trust that He has better plans for your life? Remember, He has gone ahead of you and has laid out clear markers for you.

Jesus knows how to keep your heart safe in His security and love. There are certain things we need to do, confident that He is strengthening us. One of the barriers to our freedom is unforgiveness. Forgiveness unblocks the flow of love and life and releases lightness in our spirits. I don't know of anything with a more immediate lightening effect on our hearts than forgiveness.

KEEPING IN STEP WITH THE SPIRIT

The Holy Spirit may be inviting you to have more freedom right now. Simply attend to what He is doing in your heart. Is there someone coming to mind that you want to forgive?

Consider, *How has my life been affected by them? How have other people I love been affected?* When you're ready, choose to let go of your hurt as well as what you think they might owe you.

Ask yourself, *What has my role been and how can I offer compassion and forgiveness to myself? What judgments towards people or God am I still holding in my heart? Am I willing to lay those down at the foot of the cross?*

Ask God, "*Is there something You want me to give You?*" Then ask, "*What do You give me in return?*" Say, "*Father, would You give me your perspective of my situation? Show me a wider picture of my life so that I can breathe more easily and remember Your promises to me. What do You promise me? Father, is there anything else You would like me to give You today?*"

LET'S PRAY

Father, all of who I am is in You. You are my life and my rock. There is no one else who can help me the way that You do. Come into the deep places of my heart, and lead me out to a spacious place. Show me who You are for me right now. I welcome Your comfort, Your presence, and all of who You are. Thank You that You are always with me. Your presence never leaves me, and I can enter into Your presence any time I want to. I come by faith. Whether I feel You or don't feel You, I trust that You are filling me, surrounding me, behind me, beneath me, over me, consuming me, and filling my whole home. I worship You. I love You. Thank You for Your love and that You have good plans for my life. I let go of my future, I take hold of the promises won for me on the cross, and I plant my feet in the kingdom of heaven, right here on earth. Your kingdom come, on earth as it is in heaven. Your will be done in my life. Here I am, coming to You, Father, as a child. I rest in my Jesus, and I am held in Your arms.

A BLESSING FOR YOU

I bless you with courage.
I bless you with grace to live in union with Christ.
I bless your intimacy with Him.
I bless your heart to trust the Father's goodness and His love for you.
I bless your perspective to come into alignment with thankfulness.
I bless you to be strengthened with a growing awareness of His love.
I bless you with power to surrender your heart completely to Him.
I bless you to know that He still has good plans for your life.
I bless you to live in the moment.
I bless you to love yourself.
I bless you to live from your heart.
I bless you to recognize when the season is changing and to flow into the next season as the Lord leads you.

> ***I pray that he would unveil within you the unlimited riches of his glory and favor until supernatural strength floods your innermost being.***
>
> **—Ephesians 3:16**

NINE
LOVE FALLS DOWN

The BRIDEGROOM-KING:
Oh my beloved, you are lovely. When I see you in your beauty, I see a radiant city where we will dwell as one. More pleasing than any pleasure, more delightful than any delight, you have ravished my heart, stealing away my strength to resist you. Even hosts of angels stand in awe of you. Turn your eyes from me; I can't take it anymore! I can't resist the passion of these eyes that I adore. Overpowered by a glance,
my ravished heart—undone.
—Song of Songs 6:4-5—

The yearning of my heart has always been to experience this overwhelming love of God described in the Song of Songs. His presence, which speaks of His love, I could never get enough of. In His presence, I was filled with peace, and it was amazing. The encouragement and comfort of God's presence, even in death, is stronger than any other emotion. Honestly, it became my most treasured possession. But what about the experience of pure love? I longed to look into Jesus' eyes and be completely lost in His ravishing love!

ANTICIPATION

With my grieving season freshly behind me, I gingerly and enthusiastically embraced a 9-month Iris Leader's School in central California. I took my happy dog, Simba, picked up my new roommate, and would-be good friend, Catherine, from the Seattle airport and headed down the west coast in my Rav4, bursting with houseplants, suitcases, and a Papasan chair, to our breezy oceanside city. We were greeted with a blue sky and an endless sandy beach. Having left my job, I felt free as a bird with few responsibilities and new opportunities. I changed my Facebook description from teacher to "child of God," intuitively knowing that teaching was behind me and something brand new was ahead.

> "The Father's love is a revelation. It is an experience of the substance of the love of God being put into your heart."[1] —Jordan James

---

A few months prior, I had a dream in the night that I carried with me. Not understanding the extent to which God spoke through dreams yet, I still knew that heaven had opened and I had experienced something precious. It was a dream of supernatural love, right from the heart of God, which would soon unlock true freedom of who He created me to be.

DREAM

I am in my old house that was my ex-boyfriend's home but now I live there alone. I'm with a young man named Chris, and we are chatting; it's super comfortable and relaxed. Then he asks me a simple question (I don't recall what it is). Simultaneously, I am inexplicably exploding with love and everything changes. I am wildly in love and know his love for me is the same. The quality of love was astonishing, completely consuming my heart, and it came upon me in an instant. I wake, stunned with emotion, realizing I had never experienced anything of this intensity in my life. I think to myself, "I thought I was happy being alone, but if this is love, I'm not fully living without it." This experience of love stayed with me the entire day, gradually fading into a clear, unforgettable memory. I knew the love of God touched me, but what did it mean?

I told my dream to Marie, my pastor's wife, and she said simply, "The ex-boyfriend is Brian, the young man is a sign of a new relationship, and you will meet someone this year. It will be fresh, comfortable, and relaxed. God is priming the pump." Wide-eyed, in wonderment I responded like Mary, and quietly in my heart, I said, "Lord, let it be unto me according to Your will." I had always wanted to say that!

Later, I was in a dream interpretation class, explaining my dream. I happened to be nearing the end of a long fast as well, which I had named, "Sought After." After hearing this same dream, the teacher said Jesus was calling me into experiencing His Bridegroom love for me. Chris meant "Christ," and He is asking me a question that will change everything. All night, my spirit was longing to know what the question was. I think the question is, "Will you dance with me, Chara?" I answered, "Yes," and was instantly transported into a heavenly place.

Jesus was inviting me into a bride-bridegroom relationship with Him. I was comfortable and relaxed with Jesus. But he was inviting me into an intimacy beyond what I had ever experienced, where I would know the supernatural love I felt in my dream.

As the teacher released this interpretation, I immediately was filled with an intensity of love that I had never experienced in waking life. Suddenly, I was hearing Jesus speak words of love to me, and I felt held in His embrace. In my spirit, I was carried away, and for days all I could hear were His words of love constantly spoken to me. I could go home and attend my classes the next day, but the whole time, I felt lost in this experience of being deeply loved by Jesus.

> ***We have come into an intimate experience with God's love, and we trust in the love he has for us.***
>
> **—1 John 4:16a**

Journal, Dec.8, 2014, Fast Day 38:

> *My real life is hidden with Christ in God"* (Col. 3:3).
>
> *The most beautiful thing is happening today! I am falling in love with Jesus. <3 Last night I learned my dream was first of all falling in over-the-top, unworldly love with Jesus. I think the question is so simple: "Will you dance with Me, Chara?" Is it okay for Jesus to be in love with me? There is nowhere else for me to be, nowhere else for me to go, I am simply in His arms, and He dances with me. The teacher is going on about stuff,*

but I can only dance with Jesus. I am an eternal spirit, ageless. Jesus is God. Jesus is a great new discovery for me. He is near, and I am amazed. My heart is filling with love. I want to stay in this place forever. Jesus, can I?

I will move you deeper into who I am. My everlasting joy is you, Chara. I will not grow tired or weary, and My understanding, no one can fathom. I invite you into Me, Chara. This will be a divine dance, and you are My joy. Beloved, I love who you are. Come away with me, my darling, my love. I want you to see Me, too. I want to be known by you, Chara. I created you for this romance, Chara, and you are worth waiting for. I breathe on you, Chara. This is the beginning of a new way of life for you. I embrace you. I lead you, and we will together dance through life.

Jesus, everything fades in anticipation of dancing with You, of knowing You more. This is what I've been dying for. Let me die to myself, Jesus, that I might possibly LIVE! I cannot live without being IN LOVE. Being in love with You, Jesus, is the best romance I could imagine. All other men fade in comparison to You, Jesus. I am SOO amazed that You revealed Yourself to me in that dream, and now revelation comes. Is this a special invitation?

HAHAHA! Chara, come near, nearer to Me. You are My beloved girl. I created you for romance and romance alone. My heart is romantic, too. I have fallen in love with you, and I long for you to fall in love with Me. I want us to share secrets and to live in that intimate place. My heart hurts for what your heart hurts for, and I delight in your longing for freedom and delight in simple honesty and close relationships, in beauty and grace, in laughter and fun in life.

Don't tell everyone everything, Chara. Some things are private, to be shared between you and I. That's the beauty of romance. Those looking in don't understand it. Only those experiencing it fully understand each other. Trust is built in confidentiality and loyalty. Keep our relationship pure, sparkling, and refreshing. Come away with Me, My love, My darling, to the secret place.

Over the next several days, I continued like this, walking the beach, sharing secrets, and absorbing His amazing love. In the meantime, the Christmas holidays were coming soon. I had been asking the Lord if He had someone for me to marry. I had lost count of the number of times people had prophesied a "surprise" for me. I thought it was my new guitar that I was enjoying so much. But I was still receiving the word "surprise." What more could He have for me?

I was staring at the massive rocks as the waves lapped quietly on the shore. What looked like a heron was standing alone out in the bay. Gazing at the bird for several minutes, I asked the Lord, "Is that me? Will I be alone?" To my astonishment, a huge grey bird swooped into view, and the two birds took flight together, circling and soaring with their broad wings into the sky. I looked at them in wonder and then walked back to meet my friend.

For the Spirit-wind blows as it chooses. You can hear its sound, but you don't know

> ***where it came from or where it's going. So it is within the hearts of those who are Spirit-born!***
>
> **—John 3:8**

What happened next, again, I quote from my journal:

> *January 14, 2015*
>
> *Help! I am so helpless and vulnerable; I cannot even contain myself. My heart is undone. How can this be??! Is it real? Is this Your will for me, Lord? Or have I gone off my rocker? This is not who I picked. I asked You for a ponytail! A free spirit! Does Michael have either? All he did was give me a New Year's hug on Sunday, look at me with warmth, and I got lost in his eyes and instantly fell head over heels in love. I cannot eat. I cannot sleep. The last two nights I've been awake since about 3 am. I'm going crazy. Lord Jesus, direct my heart.*

LOVE LANDED ON ME

We were at church the day before classes began in January, and yes, I fell so in love with Michael that I couldn't think straight. In a split second, love landed on me in a similar way to how I experienced the love of Jesus. He asked me how my Christmas was, gave me a quick hug, and I felt exactly the way I had in my dream: suddenly overwhelmed by an all-consuming love. It was like the heavens opened up and poured love into my heart. I stumbled back to my seat, mumbling to myself, "Jesus, come straighten this out and show me the way." Truthfully, I had seen Michael in class for four months. Others had dared suggest Michael might be someone for me, but I made it abundantly clear to them that he was not someone I would date. Catherine said that my emotional response to him went from one end of the spectrum to the other. We had not been interested in each other at all. He was reeling from his past relationships, and my observation was that to start with, he needed a makeover. I wanted to travel the world, and I sized up Michael as not being for me.

Boy, was I wrong! But I kept this secret love between Jesus and I and my roommate Catherine, completely willing at this point for everything to go away. I knew better than to trust emotion alone—wasn't I the one with endless crushes in high school? Plus, I understood marriage and what was required. At the same time, all my heart wanted was to curl up by Michael and snuggle. My rational mind was full of doubt, so I continually surrendered it to Jesus. All week, I wrestled in a fog. Tuesday, one of our teachers stood me up in class and said, "What you thought you came to this school for, God has much more for you in mind than that and a different purpose than you think. You will know; it will be evident."

A group of us were going out wine tasting on Friday, several days later. Michael had asked me to go for coffee right before in response to me asking him to tell me something interesting about himself. I had no idea what might happen. Michael was naively going out with someone hopelessly in love with him. I asked my daughter Jenna, "What will I wear? Is this a date or just a coffee?" My wise daughter replied, "Mom, wear what you'd wear if you were going out with a good friend." Relieved, I nervously waited for Michael to pick me up.

There was a glorious blue sky and warm temperatures that afternoon. Michael took me to the nearby Avila Beach where we grabbed a coffee and walked the pier. Instantly, he made me feel completely at rest. We talked easily and ended up sitting at a table with our ice cream for several hours. Michael asked about my life, and we chatted back and forth. Nothing deep or particularly personal was said. Yet we would later half-joke that somehow there must have been a portal into heaven over our heads.

SEEING WHO WE WERE CREATED TO BE

Michael explained that as I was casually speaking about my family, he was thinking to himself on a whole different level, "Whoever she thinks I am—I'm not that guy!" And then as time went by, soon he was thinking, "Maybe I am that guy!" Communication seemed to be happening in two realms at once. The natural conversation about where we grew up and then the supernatural revelation that had begun to flow in both of us. I was discovering that Michael was extremely kind and thoughtful and that he could hold a conversation.

As we stood up from our seats and walked along, I said, "I feel safe with you." Michael responded uncharacteristically by drawing me into a warm embrace just around the corner. I tried to freeze the moment, willing it not to end. I was literally speechless for the next 20 minutes, but luckily Michael was amiably chatting as we made our way to a cozy Italian place for an early dinner.

By the time evening came, we stood looking at the stars in wonder. My heart was expanding, and I was transported to another realm. Michael was wondering aloud in amazement, "There's something going on here beyond you and I. There's a purpose to us coming together, and it's beyond us."

For me, time had disappeared, and I was simply caught up in a new revelation of love. I had experienced it in my dream. It made sense that the love of Jesus was what I experienced, but for the same love to land on both of us like this was only supernatural. Michael had decided after three failed marriages that he was done with marriage. He decided God was enough for him. We didn't pick each other—God Himself landed in our hearts.

I eventually began to eat normally again and sleep through the night. I still wanted to take Michael for a haircut and shopping for new clothes, but all that didn't seem to matter anymore. My old impressions were washed away.

I asked myself, "Who is Michael?" He is someone who takes my breath away. In his arms, I come alive. I trust him and feel so safe with him. The Father said that Michael was His budding warrior for the Kingdom of Light. He will champion causes and push back darkness to create room for His Presence to flourish in people's lives. And the Father was calling me into battle with Him, using an alternatively gentle kiss and sharp sword, as needed. What a team.

> ***God is continually teaching you to unselfishly love one another.***
>
> **—1 Thessalonians 4:9**

Within five weeks, we were engaged. My daughter Jenna came from Toronto and threw a spontaneous heartwarming engagement party for us.

With Michael around, I was simply lost in love, completely abandoned to this heavenly, all-consuming experience of love.

When Michael was not with me, I did battle doubt. My main question was, *God, is this really you?* I checked and rechecked the many confirmations God had given me.

Several dreams, multiple prophetic words from strangers, the storks on the beach, and even my perfume was prophetic—"Falling in Love." All of these messages and signs helped reassure me. However, my real battle was the question, *Could God really be this good?* Michael's kindness and gentleness wrecked me every day.

Eventually, a seemingly long five months later we were married on my parents' beach in Canada in a beautiful simple celebration of what God had done. We were completely lost in love and eager to begin our lives together. What now, Lord?

Michael and I talk often of our love story, reveling in its glory. We feel honored that the Father would give us this remarkable gift. However, as time went on, we noticed that while the Lord is love, we were not Him. We were meant to protect each other's hearts, but we weren't doing it perfectly. Wherever there was a wound hidden in our hearts, there was a potential for us to press on the pain.

The first few times were a shock! An irritated look, an ignored response, or a misunderstanding turned into an escalation of emotions, as we tried to explain and defend, argue and cajole. With our hearts so wide open to each other, it was even more of a painful contrast than I'd ever experienced. The smallest inconsideration was jolting. We were supposed to be the ones who spoke endless words of love to each other for five hours endlessly on an airplane ride! We don't get angry with each other! What was this?

All that matters now is living in the faith

that is activated and brought to perfection by love.

—Galatians 5:6

I quickly realized there had to be another way. The Father was on the move again, showing me the ways of the kingdom and the stakes were high. I was listening. I focused on what I knew to be true: 1. God had given me a spectacular gift of love in Michael. 2. Michael's heart was good. Armed with these two facts and the reassurance of the Holy Spirit that we were on the right path, all I could do was listen for a new way of navigating the flurries. Although they were infrequent, we could not afford to lose this treasure.

What if I simply let the 'ouch' go? What if I gave space for imperfection? What if I didn't take offense? I soon discovered that in the moment of tension, I had a choice. I could let the comment or action fall to the ground, or I could allow it to escalate. Again, I can't help but think of people who are experts at diffusing conflict, knowing that I am still not one of them.

However, I do know how to let go and lean on the Holy Spirit for encouragement. I decided to give it a whirl. At that moment, the choice was hard! I was tempted to respond negatively, and sometimes I might, as this can be one of my weaknesses, but when I did let go, amazingly, nothing was lost; love remained in the air, and in the atmosphere of acceptance, my husband would often later apologize.

It's shocking to me how long it takes and how difficult it is to die to self and really allow love in. However, the battle is so worth it. For in the midst of love, we find safety to be our true self. Marriage at its best is a beautiful reflection of the passionate love of God for us. I want to be an example of love for Michael and also rest in his love for me. We are thankful the Father put us together and excited to have just celebrated our 5th wedding anniversary (as of 2020).

UPSIDE DOWN & INSIDE OUT

Interestingly, just after we were married, I had a dream that my yellow airplane dropped from the sky and was only a couple feet off the ground. I had to land. Devastated, I was pushing my plane along the road into town along a lake.

I met a man who said, "What's wrong?"

"My plane is broken," I cried, "and I don't know how to get it in the air again!"

"Don't worry," he said. "My friend, Joe Parish, will get your plane working again."

Wow. I was so relieved and thankful that God still had good plans for me, and I could trust Him to lead me into them.

The Father was continuing to tend to my heart. While my plane was grounded, I had so much more to discover. What does love look like? Is it dependent upon my behavior? How do Michael and I accept each other as we are? How do I accept myself? What keeps me from receiving love? How do we imperfectly love an imperfect person? Can we access the Father's love continually?

Incredibly, Jesus never lets go of our hand. He came to lead us directly to the Father who has all the answers. Here we were, ready to do anything He wanted us to do, but I was surprised again by the journey He took us on. Turns out, when I was looking to DO more, He was teaching me to BE more. Where I wanted to give, He wanted me to receive. Where I wanted to find life in the extraordinary, the Father was showing me His glory in the ordinary. I was learning how to embrace my weakness and trust in who He is in me. In light of this, my dream of ministry was about to be turned upside down and inside out.

LIVING FROM THE WRONG TREE

James Jordan describes the root of our need to perform, going all the way back to the two trees in the Garden of Eden:

> The Tree of the Knowledge of Good and Evil is the basis for performance-orientation and performance anxiety. Living out of that, if I'm not perfect then I'm not OK. Our worth is directly tied to our performance. We judge ourselves harshly, and by the same measuring stick, we judge others harshly. You cannot judge yourself harshly without judging the other harshly and vice versa.[2]

God's thoughts and assessments flow from His heart of love. This is something that we can so easily miss. We need to be feeding on life rather than trying to work everything out. We can be free of worrying whether or not things are up to standard. If we live from the heart, connected to the Tree of Life, there is no need to be concerned with those things. It would be a huge relief just to be free of the compulsion to judge and to then come into the life that flows from the heart of God. That is the real Gospel—to be connected to the life! What a relief and joy to be in a place of having an open heart, moving in and with the heart of love that is in God, free from having to be constantly on our toes, assessing numerous spiritual decisions and issues every minute.[3]

LOVE IS THE STANDARD

Letting go of judgment has been a steady process, one that has come in various revelations over time. I'm still in process, but moving from living under condemnation to a place of rest and approval has been an exciting and rewarding road. It began one morning when I had asked Jesus to show me the story of His love for me. He showed me so many moments of my life, and each time, He was encouraging me, cheering me on, singing over me, listening peacefully, blessing and strengthening me, and passionately loving me. He didn't hold back His emotions, but freely expressed Himself. When I was loving my babies, He was loving them with me. In the anguish of my regret, He was singing over me. He was united with me throughout my life. I thought to myself, "I'm starting to get the idea. The standards I've set for myself have been a false system of bringing love and approval."

There really is no "standard." It's because LOVE is the standard. What does love do? What does love say? If I bring a message in love, how will I bring it? LOVE brings it. Love serves it up. Love plans with hope. Love encourages. Love corrects. Love works out all things. Love equips. Love worships. Love exalts others above ourselves. Love delights in people. Love accepts ourselves and others as we are. Love doesn't demand or force. Love lets go and doesn't control. Love is the standard I need to live by. Comparing how I live or how someone else lives to any other standard is not my place.

This idea brought immediate relief yet complete confusion at the same time. To what degree do we let go of our standards and expectations of other people? Is it ever okay to blame? Is that even possible? Is it helpful? What about struggling with independence?

The one thing I know is that living from love is a much higher way to live. It means letting go of controlling not only other people but also my own life and its assessments. If I go back to the way that Jesus was looking at my entire life, He wasn't worrying about how well I did at something or getting angry at my failures. His heart was full of true love.

> ***I love each of you with the same love that the Father loves me. You must continually let my love nourish your hearts.***
>
> **—John 15:9**

Loving ourselves includes accepting our weaknesses, our challenging areas, and not expecting perfection. I've learned to give myself a break, and I've started celebrating mistakes just because I can. In Christ, I am His beloved—adored and cherished—words I'm only beginning to receive. There is so much room to grow.

I'm most excited about this because it is such a relief not to have to assess other people. I can trust the Father knows what is going on, and He's got it covered. He will let me know if I need to do anything. If He does, I know it will look and sound like love, encouragement, and inspiration. In my efforts, I often don't get it right, but this is a part of growing. The challenge is to let go.

God is love! Those who are living in love are living in God, and God lives through them.

—John 4:16b

Is it possible for us to live like that? I have found it helpful to understand what the Bible means when it says that Jesus came as the second Adam. Very simply, it means that He came to undo what Adam did and restore us into a relationship with the Father. Being restored to the Father for eternity, we eat from the tree of life. Our understanding of the tree of the knowledge of good and evil is erased as a lesser way of living. We let go of comparing and evaluating everyone. In its place, we act out of love.

The one thing that never fails is love. If you eat from the Tree of Life you will naturally have grace for people and be able to forgive them. You will be patient and kind towards them and act correctly towards them. If your perspective is that you automatically see the things that are wrong in another person's life, then you are eating from the wrong tree. If your natural default is to see things wrong in your own life, then you are eating from the wrong tree. The only Christian life that actually works is the one that flows from the Tree of Life.[4]

Marriage is the perfect place to practice this. It's difficult, no question about it. However, living in turmoil and without love is difficult, too. Even as I write this, my heart understands the struggle and the cost involved with letting go. We were never meant to do it alone. However, each time that I do let go, it has been worth it. Once I knew in my heart that I'm loved by Jesus, He gives me value, and I cannot be devalued by how anyone speaks or acts towards me. Therefore, I can let something go that hurt my feelings. I don't have to defend myself. Slowly, I can live from love in the places where I am healed and not threatened.

However, in the places where I am still hurt, I need more love. I communicate these the best I can with as much clarity as I can. I am not perfect. I am allowed to love myself with the same ability I have to love others. I can let go of the so-called standards I have for myself and let love be the standard I live from. I can speak encouragingly to myself. I can allow myself to make mistakes without accusation. I forgive myself. I practice loving myself and joining as one with Jesus.

If love is my standard, I have no fear of being rude or selfish because that wouldn't be love. I don't worry about becoming careless because I delight in beauty and excellence wherever they matter to me. However, priorities may differ between days and circumstances and seasons. Maybe everyone gets to choose how they want to live their lives. Cultural norms bear a lot of weight. However, we live in the kingdom of God, where love is the currency, and everything is measured by love. Perhaps we need to put all our attention on love.

James Jordan describes it so well:

> You don't get peace by doing the right thing as a Christian. You get peace by forgetting about what is right and wrong and falling into His love. When you fall into His love you will get filled with it and you will be able to do nothing else but love - and love cannot sin.[5]

For those of us who are inspired by entering into other's experiences, here is another intimate entry from my journal, where I recorded what I heard Jesus speaking to me. Everyone is invited into His heart, so be blessed.

Jan 1, 2018

> *Come dance.*
>
> *Who you are to Me is a dream. You are a dream I had of one woman so gracious in beauty, in her spirit, in her physical body, and in her soul—her mind and personality. My dream was My joy, and I created you. You were born for my pleasure. I delight in you—all your thoughts, the way your mind moves, and encompasses your emotions at the same time. Your beauty is a fragrance—sweet spikenard united with meadow flowers and citrus. I am your love and you are Mine. Purity is written on your forehead. You wear a white dress with a tie around your waist, and it free flows the way you do. You are a danger in the spirit, Chara, and you are destined for heavenly places. Your fragrance goes ahead of you, and the angels are all excited together with me. The world is aching and groaning for such a time as this. Open wide your mouth, and I will fill it. You need not prepare what to say; you need to dance with Me in the secret place.*
>
> *I am pleased with you. This was your time to rest, to bask in the lover I gave you. This was your time to glory in the goodness of My heart for you. Be peaceful, quiet, calm in your spirit, your soul, and your body. I designed this season of glory as a blessing for you. You needed it,*

and it was also your reward for your faithfulness to Me. I've been very active during this time though, preparing for this next upcoming season in your life. Adventure is only the beginning. Unfathomable intimacy is where I'm drawing you—into the depths of My heart.

Come.

TEN
HOME

You live fully in Me and now I live fully in them so that they will experience perfect unity, and the world will be convinced that You have sent Me, for they will see that You love each one of them with the same passionate love that You have for Me.
—John 17:23—

"It's one thing to know Father loves you. It's another thing to know he's loving you right now."[1]
—Helene King—

One morning I thought I heard God ask me if I wanted to know the plans He had for my life. Startled, I put my coffee cup down and picked up my pen, eagerly wondering what He would say. I saw the outline of a region or country, and I heard, "You will feel at home here," followed by a quiet whisper, "Tanzania." I was in awe. Not knowing anything about Tanzania, I immediately "Googled" it, only to discover it had everything I had ever hoped to experience in Africa—a simple village life, over 100 tribes (including Masai warriors), and all the wilderness you could imagine.

Several years later, I am married to Michael, and we decided to travel around Tanzania on a listening journey, inviting the Holy Spirit to guide our steps. I remember winding down in Stonetown, on the island of Zanzibar, and reflecting on our month-long adventure.

We spent a starry evening mingling with vendors at the night market and enjoying chicken kabobs, local Urojo soup, and fresh sugar cane juice. We had begun our travels inland in Shinyanga, where we were hosted by a new friend, who kindly invited us into his home. We shared a traditional meal and prayed for his beautiful wife. God healed something deep in her heart, and she was so excited that we were asked to pray for her family in Mwanza. Happily, we prayed for his mom, who had a dream that night about her son in heaven and spent the night joyfully dancing and shouting uncontainably in a new gift of tongues. Next, we prayed for the sister, who had tuberculosis and HIV, along with her two children. We delighted in moving around the country, meeting wonderful people and walking into unknown villages, simply following our hearts.

One day, we wandered along a red dirt road in the lush green village of Marangu, near Mount Kilimanjaro. As we walked up a narrow pathway, we saw a boy smearing on mud to repair a wall of their mud and stick home. Immediately welcoming us to sit on log stools, the family was delighted to have us pray for them though they could not understand English. We experienced the presence of Holy Spirit and left the blessing of some money for the grandmother. My heart broke with compassion for her painful joints, and I wondered at how little we could do for her.

While there, I had a dream of a black man in a military uniform inviting me onto his horse. I wondered if God was inviting us back to Tanzania. Considering the easy flow in the spirit of our listening trip, 7 months later we went back to Tanzania for a longer term. Determined again to follow the Spirit and join God wherever He was working, we suddenly found that every door we assumed we would be going through was closed. Our passion was healing prayer ministry. Since the Lord had brought so much healing to my heart followed by joy and love, I wanted to pray with others, but I was blocked in my spirit. It either fell flat or people said no.

I was a teacher and loved to plan, create lessons, and teach students. I especially loved to teach the amazing things of the Spirit of God and help people grow in their relationship with Him. While initially there was some enthusiasm, in my spirit I felt little anointing, so I stopped teaching and waited for direction.

Being flexible, I tried to consider where there was a sense of life. My heart filled with happiness as I walked along and made eye contact with the people I passed. After waiting decades to fulfill this dream, chatting with the Lord about living here in Africa was so much fun. The simple life of picking lemons off the lemon tree in the morning, walking up the road to buy sugar, and then making homemade lemon curd was rewarding. Buying fresh milk from the farmer and boiling it with salt, adding vinegar, and squeezing it in a cheesecloth produced the most delicious paneer cheese. Bartering in the open-air market with the youth, buying new shoes for all the students, and dressing up for a dance party was a memorable and fun event, complete with the novelty of homemade cake and meat skewers. Being friends with people and sharing our lives, our struggles, our days with each other was where I discovered life. Could it be so simple? And so we joined Him there, living life and simply loving the people around us.

Generally, quiet and peaceful days reigned, yet the atmosphere felt charged from acts of random desperation as well. On occasion, chaos would intermittently explode. On a hot afternoon, the naive gas attendant put diesel instead of unleaded gas into our vehicle and it broke down. A sweltering day was spent solving the problem, relying on kind strangers to help, waiting for hours and hours, and eating fries and freshly chopped watermelon in the heat of the day.

Another day, the city authorities arrived at the NGO base where we were staying to shut it down based on ridiculous lies they had heard. An extensive meeting was called to sort it out. Chaos also came in the dark of night as we were returning home after a celebration dinner with supporters from the USA. Stopping for a motorbike blocking our street, suddenly, a masked robber opened the driver's car door and in a flurry of commotion stole my friend's wallet full of recent donations to her ministry.

These acts only revealed the desperation people were carrying —desperation for security, for love and belonging, for comfort, for hope, for peace, for acceptance, for understanding, and, above all, desperation for money for food, for school, and for whatever people believed would give them happiness, respect, and security. I noticed this, and I felt peace myself, but I felt so limited, even helpless, to offer much at all.

The mission organization we were with provided food and clothes for persecuted youth with albinism and helped them prepare for independent living. It was wonderful. Yet in my heart, there was so much more I wanted to give. I longed to enter with these youth into the presence of God, the flow of His Spirit, His comfort, and His pure love that would heal the trauma locked in these beautiful hearts. I knew His love would enter into painful memories and evaporate shame and guilt. His love would undo unworthiness and release value and belonging into hearts. We can deeply know that we are loved because He loves us. I wanted to share His freedom in being accepted as we are, included in the family of God. These are the important things I wanted these youth with albinism to experience for themselves. It would be a strong foundation upon which they could build their lives. From this place of being securely loved by God, hearts would open and life would flow.

Why then couldn't I do this? Somehow I felt stuck. On the other hand, the Holy Spirit was showing me something about the beauty of ordinary life. I experienced life in simple greetings and friendly banter. Was this enough? While He had taught me Himself about what He could do through prayer, now He was showing me something new. My husband began to read aloud to me a revelation that both of us instantly knew God was leading us into. This is James Jordan's book, *Ancient Road*:

> Jesus said that His yoke is easy and His burden is light. I do not believe there is any freedom, joy or rest except in the love of the Father. We have been living a Christianity that is handicapped by a lack of revelation of the Father. To put it simply, we have been living a Christianity based on two revelations;

> the revelation of Jesus as Saviour and Lord, and the revelation of the Holy Spirit's indwelling. This is like trying to balance on a two-legged stool. To put it another way, the foundation of our Christianity is incomplete. Something vital is missing. To date, we have had only a conceptual understanding rather than a revelation of the Father. What is more, we have had a flawed understanding of who the Father is.[2]

The Holy Spirit was opening my eyes to a new level of love that was available. I had always wanted to experience the love of the Father! Loving Jesus was amazing. Experiencing the Holy Spirit in deep ways was incredible, but now He was leading me to a new place. I had not arrived, had not even come close, but my heart recognized this longing, and I knew it would bring me into a new freedom.

OUR MOST VALUABLE GIFT

I realized with clarity that the love of the Father pouring into our hearts must be our most valuable gift. If we're not experiencing His love, what have we to give? Jesus came so that we would live in abundance and know inexpressible joy and absolute freedom. He said it was for freedom that He set us free through His death on the cross. So where is the freedom? How do we stay in joy? Why isn't love consuming us and flowing out of our hearts towards our friends and enemies?

In Tanzania, all these thoughts came to a head. In this tension, it was clear that I needed to be experiencing the river of life on a deeper level because that in itself would be a valuable gift. I don't believe in making things happen on my own. When the Spirit moves, His power is evident. After all I had been through, I recognized when I was in the flow of the Spirit that would move mountains and when I wasn't. My husband and I both saw that we needed a deeper revelation of God's love—one that would break new barriers.

How could we encounter the Father's love in our hearts? We soaked up the book we were reading and immediately researched opportunities to learn more. "Where can we experience this?" We wondered. Before we knew it, we were at a three-month school, more like a retreat, called "Inheriting the Nations" on a remote island in New Zealand with Fatherheart Ministries. The purpose was to experience the love of the Father and a deeper revelation of sonship.

As James Jordan explains:

> As we have come to experience the love of the Father, our perspective on many things is changing. One of these things, for example, is that the centrality of the heart becomes an issue of fundamental importance. When you are not experiencing love, all that you possess is mostly knowledge. But love can only be experienced in your heart. Your heart needs to be open to receive love. You can have a new teaching about love, but it takes an experience in your heart to receive the actuality of love.
>
> As we begin to experience Him loving us more and more, our hearts come into sharper focus. The condition of our heart is put under a magnifying glass, and we begin to realize how important the heart really

> is. As a result, we are finding that many things regarding how we understand Christianity are changing quite dynamically. This is the crux of it. It is not merely that your heart is important. The reality is that your heart is vital because it is your heart that is changing. Knowledge is something that is of the mind, but understanding is an issue of the heart.[3]

The Lord had our complete attention. Right at the start, I saw a fence with everything God had done behind it. I knew I was to let go of all He had done for now and vulnerably receive what He had for me, simply as a little girl. That alone revealed to me the extent that I based my value on what He had done for me, rather than on who He is or who I am to Him. Boy, I had much to learn. Thankfully, the glory of what it means to be a beloved daughter has been exploding in my spirit since then, and the wonder of who Father is and who He created me to be is unfolding in spectacular light.

This revelation of being fathered by a perfect Father who abides in me is rooted in God making His home in me. Home is where it all happens, right in our hearts. *Father, open the eyes of our hearts, so that we can see You and know You.*

WHAT IS HOME?

What is home? For a traveler like me, there are levels of what feels like home. There's my country, Canada, where I understand the cultural innuendos and relax in a way that's noticeable compared to even being in the United States. I cross the border on my way home, and my shoulders relax just a tad. I watch the Canadian forest meadows for bears and take in the cool fresh mountain air, enjoying the familiar landscape. Even meeting a Canadian around the world brings immediate camaraderie because we understand each other on a level unique to being a Canadian. I tend to feel right at home meeting other Canadians when I travel. Often, we might interpret the culture we are visiting in a similar way. Actually, I thrive on breathing in the atmosphere of a bustling culture full of new sounds, unique smells, and a cultural rhythm that alerts my senses, as well as my curiosity, but there's nothing like home.

Then there's feeling at home in my city where I have my favorite coffee shops, according to my moods. I take the shortcut across the tracks and through the alley on my way to the park walkway. I recognize the seasonal changes, and my behavior instinctively adapts with the weather—gathering in front of the warm fireplace in winter and around a beach campfire in summer.

Perhaps home is primarily the house we live in. When you arrive home, what kind of emotion does that evoke? Do you feel accepted? Are you loved? I remember the balloons and paper decorations we would place all over the house so that my children would wake up on their birthdays, knowing they were celebrated. I think of home as a place where I can relax, take off my shoes, and allow my facial expressions to match the reality of my heart. I'm not on guard at home. It's actually a place to retreat from the world for a while. I can open the fridge and eat what I want. The decor is a reflection of what I like and even who I am, at least in a compromise with the others living in my home. To the best of my ability, home is my safe place in the world. For those of us where home is not our safe place, this is traumatic, and we long for this safety. We know how home should be.

While we hope to find authenticity and confidence to be ourselves in our homes, to various degrees, home never actually meets our hopes and expectations. Home is the place where we might receive our deepest wounds because we all parent out of our brokenness. From childhood and throughout our whole lives, these wounds are either forming or in process of healing.

It's not a perfect home we live in. In spite of our best family experiences, our longing for a perfect home remains. We know intuitively that we were born to be loved. We expect a home to be an atmosphere of acceptance, belonging and trust—our safe place. Even in its imperfection, our heart still recognizes home as a place where we live.

After a long trip, I always breathe a sigh of relief as I kick off my shoes and flop on my bed. This need for comfort sits in the center of who we are, and our lives come and go from whatever stability and support home provides.

> ***I promise that I will never leave you helpless or abandon you as orphans—I will come back to you! And my Father will love you so deeply that we will come to you and make you our dwelling place.***
>
> **—John 14:18, 23**

It's interesting how Jesus spoke of home, in this case translated as dwelling place. He said that WE WILL COME TO YOU AND MAKE YOU OUR DWELLING PLACE. "We" means the Father, Jesus, and the Holy Spirit. Everything in the world is limited in what it can give us. But the home that Jesus, the Father, and the Holy Spirit make in us is limitless in its capacity. *ABIDE in Me, and I will ABIDE in you,* Jesus also said.

The safe place that our hearts need is found right inside of us. Home is not far; it is surprisingly near, and we have full access here in our hearts to the heart of God. He is our source, the one who knows how to comfort us and meet our every need. Home is where I can let down my hair and take off my makeup. With transparency, I can snuggle into the love of God and let Him Father me. I am a child—His child.

NO STRIVING

Without effort or striving, I am known, I am seen, and I am understood. I am only beginning to marvel at what this means for my life. It has been an entirely new way of living for me. Without the need for striving, there is room to explore who I am. What do I like to do? Love opens my heart; acceptance draws me out. This is what Jesus meant when He said They would make Their home in us.

I have also been surprised at what I am free to let go of as I experience more love. Recently, it almost feels like I keep growing younger and younger. Since I have closed the door on my identity as a teacher, and sought after living as a child of my Father, I have noticed that I am also letting go of what I know. It's like I'm starting all over again with the heart of a child. I'm holding His hand and chatting to Him as we walk through the day. "Here I am!" I say aloud, several times a day. I almost feel like I'm playing hide and seek as a 2-year-old who naively gives away their hiding spot in their eagerness to be found. I want to be found—picked up, thrown in the air, played with, seen for the ageless beauty that He created me for and not the wrinkles reflected in my mirror. I want to see who I am as reflected in His eyes.

THERE IS NONE LIKE YOU

In my heart, home is where I am seen. To the degree I know I am seen, I feel accepted by God. One afternoon after class in New Zealand, I looked up to find my classmate, Anne-Marie, looking silently into my eyes. Wondering at her purpose, I gazed back and waited. I saw she was communicating something but wrestled for a minute with whether she was asking me something or simply resting in what God was doing. Feeling completely comfortable, I held her gentle gaze for several minutes, slowly recognizing joy and love in her eyes. Eventually, she expressed how the Father's love for me was welling up in her heart and how beautiful He said I was. A bit taken aback that God would not only think that but also show someone else, I later sat on my bed, pondering this. I thought to myself, "I wonder what Father sees when He looks at me?"

Walking up to my dresser mirror, I looked into my green eyes. They looked back at me, reflecting vulnerable openness. I heard a song flowing through my mind, "There is none like you. No one else can touch my heart like you do; I could search for all eternity long, and find—there is none like you!"

Suddenly, revelation burst out of my heart. The secret to our relationship was in my uniqueness! Because I am unique, I am irreplaceable and highly valued. The amazing thing about revelation is that once it is released, everything else I think or used to think has to line up with what I now know. The shift in my understanding was permanent. My value is secure because I am unique.

I already know that whatever God creates is good. Now I understand that He sees me with adoration. I am eternal in my spirit, beautiful beyond words, unique, irreplaceable, and important. All of Abba's creations are extraordinary—stunning in beauty! I am adored beyond my wildest dreams. Certainly, I have much to discover about who I really am.

REST

As Father is showing me what it means to be seen and valued, I am beginning to realize that Home is not a house, a city, or a country. It is a place inside of me where I dwell in Christ with my Father and the Holy Spirit. Wherever I am, He is with me, always my safe place. I can see that my image of Him making His home in me is changing. My heart is feeling more spacious; there is room to stretch, to explore, and to breathe deeply. I am entering into a deeper sense of rest than I have ever known. Who knew!? I thought I understood about living in peace, but as I believe what Father says, I also allow myself to be valued, and a quiet rest permeates my soul.

It wasn't until my heart felt safe that I could really tell what was inside. One reason it didn't feel safe is because I was living in self-condemnation for so long that I was holding myself a prisoner. All negative thinking kept me under lock and key. Learning how God thinks by looking at how Jesus thought has been so freeing. He is always full of grace, confident in hope, and faithful to help me. How wonderful to know that in Christ I can relax, because I am accepted as I am.

What a joy it is to be called, "Mom." I can see why God chose to be the Father! No wonder He is bursting with joy with all His children. However, I messed up, too. Usually, I was trying too hard and didn't know enough to understand I needed to stop and do the opposite. I understand in my head that we only know what we know, but my heart wouldn't let myself off the hook. Memories would surface, and sorrow rolled over in my heart in regret for mistakes I had made. I felt I deserved punishment. I lived with this cry in my heart, "How could I have hurt my own children that I love?!"

JESUS HAS GOT ME COVERED

It was only in the atmosphere of acceptance and belonging that I learned that not only was I going to be making mistakes, but that it was okay. Jesus has got me covered. Of course I don't want to give myself grace because the consequences are hard to live with. But if I couldn't offer grace to myself, could I really offer it to anyone? The option of showing kindness, forgiveness, acceptance to myself suddenly felt so appealing. If love is all that is important, then I can love myself enough to make room for mistakes.

For years, I've tried to understand this, but finally I agreed with Jesus: it is finished. I listed all my sorrows and was shocked to discover that I had been tormenting myself over eleven mistakes. Considering the weight they had taken up in my heart I thought there had been many more than that after a lifetime of parenting. I dropped them one by one, as rocks off of my imaginary boat, and forgave myself. This too was a turning point for me and the beginning of understanding a new level of union with Jesus as He promised in Matthew 11:28-30:

> ***Are you weary, carrying a heavy burden? Then come to me. I will refresh your life, for I am your oasis. Simply join your life with mine. Learn my ways and you'll discover***

> ***that I'm gentle, humble, easy to please. You will find refreshment and rest in me. For all that I require of you will be pleasant and easy to bear.***

STILLNESS

Proof of newfound freedom to be myself became apparent when I gathered at home with my family after returning from New Zealand. My sister commented on a good idea she had for my hairstyle. We chatted easily in the kitchen. This is how we live, always sharing ideas and thoughts, ready to give advice on the important things of life, such as hair, clothes, and shoes. Almost nothing is taboo. Having two amazing sisters, we always have much to talk about, but this time my reaction was completely different than what I was used to. What was happening?

Inside my belly, I felt complete rest. It was a brand new feeling that I call stillness. No stirring of anticipation for a new hairstyle idea. No questions for her or wondering about options but just perfect peace. I didn't feel compelled or even interested to consider her idea, and it wasn't because I loved my hairstyle. At that moment, it just didn't matter to me. Being seen, known, valued, and comforted had given me new security so that I didn't rely on others' opinions for approval. That stillness was a sign for me of coming to a new level of acceptance. I felt secure and could look people comfortably in the eye. Here inside my heart is where I can simply be myself, without trying. I was home.

Knowing that I belong is something I take with me wherever I go. No one can take it from me. There is a strength that comes from accepting myself that is deeper than I have known before. I may get nervous in new situations, and I am learning much about who I am and beginning to stretch myself. I think that's okay. If I'm scared or get something all wrong, that's okay, too. My heart will still get hurt, and offense might pop up. What I have discovered is that life is more than getting things right.

What is right? It's actually being authentic and enjoying the moments of life, walking down the street and connecting warmly with the woman selling bananas on the corner or smiling at the tailor working on my new skirt. It is knowing when to let go of a concern and when to speak encouragement to someone.

If the Father hasn't expected me to be at a certain standard, but continually is teaching me new things, then who am I to judge? When new hurts are exposed in my heart, then I try not to be defensive. If I want to motivate and encourage others, I need to start with being gentle and kind to myself. I cannot give what I do not have.

Home is a place of authenticity and significance that comes from being loved by the Father. I belong here—in my own heart, as a little girl, adored by her Papa.

ELEVEN

FREE TO BE ME

For the Spirit-wind blows as it chooses.
You can hear its sound, but you don't know where it
came from or where it's going.
So it is within the hearts of those
who are Spirit-born!
—John 3:8—

"There comes a day when you're gonna look around and
realize happiness is where you are."[1]
—Chief Tui—

My heart sings when I think of the princess chief Moana, naively and courageously jumping on her raft and crossing the reef barrier into unknown waters to meet her destiny. She thought beyond the dangers to herself and risked all to follow her passion. As she went, the ocean helped her. I believe we can trust our hearts to find the path where true life will meet us.

When our hearts are closed in self-protection from being battered and bruised, it's hard to trust what's inside until we spend time in healing. However, planted within our hearts is a true God-given desire for significance and freedom to be ourselves. Here we find meaning and purpose, doing what we were destined to do. I think it will feel natural—like something we were born to do—if only we can get past the reef.

Discovering our identity as a son or daughter of our Father is the key which will unlock who we are so that we will have the courage to go beyond the reef and live the abundant life that Jesus promised, beyond all we could ask or imagine.

> ***I have come to give you everything in abundance, more than you expect—life in its fullness until you overflow!***
>
> **—John 10:10b**

It's one thing to believe we are a son or daughter of God, but it's something else entirely to experience the Father's love. I have known the love of Jesus and the presence of the Holy Spirit, but until I felt the Father's love in my heart, I knew I was missing the main thing. The power that would infuse me with confidence in who I am was the love of the Father. I know this because of the dynamic relationship that Jesus had as a Son to His Father. He revealed to us who the Father was:

> ***You are my righteous Father, but the unbe-***

> ***lieving world has never known you in the perfect way that I know you! And all those who believe in me also know that you have sent me! I have revealed to them who you are and I will continue to make you even more real to them...***
>
> **—John 17:25-26a**

I read those words, and my heart jumps, responding, "I want to know You in the perfect way Jesus knows you!" How can we know Father and experience His love?

I know that the Father pursues us, like the shepherd who goes out to look for his lost sheep, so that we will know His love. His relationship with us is His priority. His relationship with each one of us is so unique that it is impossible to understand how He would meet with someone else, but He did give me a glimpse into this.

With my heart held as open to Him as I knew how, I gently sought His love, without begging, but simply believing He was at work in my heart. As time went on, I noticed that keeping my heart open meant that insecurities started rising up. Walking into a large dining hall, my eyes darted around looking for a table where I might feel welcome to sit. I wasn't used to this level of vulnerability. I didn't self-comfort by telling myself what I knew in my head to be true, such as, "Of course people will want to sit with you." Rather, I let my heart reveal what needed healing. This was new territory for me, and it was uncomfortable. All I knew to do was rest my head on the Father's chest and wait for what He would do.

The feeling of being disconnected began to grow over the next few weeks. I began to feel emotional separation from my new friends, the staff, my friends and family back home, and even from my husband. Still, I did nothing but trust that Father was on the move.

MY GREAT SADNESS

One afternoon, I was sitting with God in a reading nook with a couple of other people nearby quietly writing or reading. A wave of sadness started filling me so much so that I began to be consumed by it. Staying with the sadness, it intensified until I saw myself falling, falling, falling deeply into a dark tunnel, completely disconnected from everyone. My face felt wet from crying, but I silently let it unfold. With the understanding of healing prayer that God had taught me, I could have started asking questions, but I felt to do nothing. So I stayed in the sadness until gradually it faded away.

Within the next couple of days, we had an insightful teaching by James Jordan on the Father's love based on The Gospel of John Chapter 17. He described how a father would rather take on their child's pain themselves than watch a child suffer. As a parent, this is easy to understand. This is the pain that Father felt when Jesus went to the cross.

His love for you and I was so great that He was willing to watch His own Son suffer so that we would be brought into Their love. It was the only way. And how much did Jesus suffer? More than we can comprehend: emotional humiliation, physical torture, and what felt like spiritual separation from His Father for the first time. The Father has done absolutely everything for us to be brought back into the relationship that He designed us to live in from the beginning. His sacrifice was the greatest there was. There is nothing else.

WAVES OF LOVE

When I went to sleep, my spirit was filled with waves of love ebbing and flowing through me all through the night. Every so often I came to partial awareness where the truths of what I had just received impressed themselves on my mind. "The Father had sacrificed all... He sent His son in His place... I am loved... He did it for me." I remember these waves of love filling me every hour or so until morning. When I woke, I was stunned. The Father had come to me and imparted His love! I had experienced my Father's love for me. I was filled with the Spirit and quietly delighted in His love. I didn't dare even speak with anyone, for I was on holy ground and didn't want to break the flow.

I decided that before class started I would read through *John 17* again. Riveted by my new revelation, I soaked in every word. When I got to verse 26, I read: ***"So that they may experience the same endless love that You have for Me, for Your love will now live in them, even as I live in them!"***

It was like a well burst forth inside of me as I read the words, "Your love will now live in them," and my heart said, "Father's love will now live in Chara." The well was overflowing with tears that could not be stopped as I floated into class. We were just about to launch into another stunning revelation of being welcomed into our new land.

NEW LAND

New land is a powerful metaphor used in the Bible. The children of Israel were in the desert for forty years before they entered the Promised Land. This was the land flowing with milk and honey that God had set apart for them. They had to fortify their cities and fight battles to defend the land; however, God was with them with victorious strategies.

The events of our lives build upon each other as the Father leads us to open up to Him. It wasn't until my heart felt safe that I could really allow what was inside to surface. Ultimately, feeling disconnected from everyone was resolved with the Father's love flowing through me. I cannot explain how it happened, but once I felt connected with His love, the feeling of disconnect didn't resurface again. The neediness inside of me, the reliance on connecting with people instead of God, simply disappeared. I began to rest in this deep security of being loved by Him that was allowing me to feel full inside.

You are always and dearly loved by God!

—Colossians 3:12

Protecting this new land has been important, too. Being careful to keep my treasures close to my heart and not throwing my pearls carelessly around is part of a new confidence. I am beginning to have a new appreciation for living life the way I want to. I am trying to resist cultural expectations and consider carefully the choices I think I can live with. I'm trying my best to let the Father lead me and not be so impulsive. I trust my heart more than before, and I am drawn to whatever gives me life.

You never know what might spark your heart, especially as security rises. I spied a huge slab of live edge fir being sold on our local marketplace. It was 12 feet long by 3 feet wide by 3 inches thick. I thought to myself, "I bet that would make an extraordinary table." Even though I did not know how to make a table, I asked the guy to cut it to 8 feet long, borrowed my son-in-law's sander, and began.

I sat with the Father on top of this rough cut slab for two weeks, vibrating all day long. The mailman, mechanic, and neighbors all stopped by to admire my work. It has the softest, smoothest finish I have ever seen, and I love running my hands over the top of it. I installed some nice iron square legs that I custom ordered and now it's a beautiful and spacious gathering place in our living area.

As I see signs of new life sparking in my spirit, I'm allowing them room to breathe. Everything else I try to limit. I don't have time for obligation, although I enjoy showing love to others in helpful ways. Is it my destiny to be a woodworker? I have also delighted in making massive 12 foot wide barn doors and various shelves. So, perhaps I am. More likely though, creativity was released in me as I discovered new security and the freedom that comes with it.

Creativity has increased in value for me as I have realized how much life it brings. It seems to me, the joy is not at all proportional to the product. Self-acceptance has made all the difference. I'm not comparing myself to others but simply enjoying expressing myself—I've noticed children do this. What seemed risky before feels less risky and more fun now.

COOKING CREATIVELY

Speaking of fun, I've abandoned recipes and enjoy pushing the limits in cooking imaginatively. I love to delight in small things, such as making delicious sourdough bread—baking with sourdough has a way of taking over my whole day! Making time for this means not being too rushed or too busy. I have slowed my life down incredibly. What's happening is that I am rested and quiet inside. I love my perspective of life. As I watch what comes out of my heart, I learn more about who I am and how I might reflect my Father.

> ***And as Christ himself is seen for who he really is, who you really are will also be revealed, for you are now one with him in his glory!***
>
> **—Colossians 3:4**

Recently, I have come to another place I am so excited about. It's about being kind and gentle with myself. Yes, it's about time! I often snuggle into my Papa's chest and allow Him to love me there. My quiet times are often wordless. It sometimes helps to come as a young child. As a good Father, He is always encouraging me; I don't have to fear disapproval or disappointment. It's not in His nature!

This freedom in my spirit has always been the longing of my heart. I am coming back to the freedom I had when backpacking through Europe, but this time, with a heart that's been through the fire. It's been through the lonely wilderness, the confusion, the doubt, and battles that were won and lost. Amid the raging storms of marriage or the slow drizzle of waiting for an opportunity, I can say that it's been a beautiful heart adventure of a different, and often difficult, kind.

A RARE GEM OF WISDOM

Sorrow is its own medicine. Truly becoming who we are, meaning who God originally created us to be, is crafted in the challenging places where we come face to face with our shortcomings. Our lives are meant to be this way—a glimpse of freedom, complete with a taste of pure joy and delight in following our hearts, followed by recognizing our limitations.

These tastes are important for spurring us on and keeping hope afloat. Our hearts return to these experiences, helping to keep our eyes on the vision of freedom to be ourselves and believing that we are truly born for this wonderful glory right here on earth, in this lifetime. Allowing sorrow to form my heart has been a rare gem of wisdom, for nothing else permeates my heart as readily as pain. I have found that moving with pain, rather than pushing it away or avoiding it, allows the Father to mold my heart. I can ask Him what He is showing me and not be afraid of what I see.

Acceptance of my weaknesses, insecurities, or occasional anxieties that may still pop up, has become part of loving myself. In the midst of love, I don't have anything to prove. I'm not valued based on my weaknesses or strengths but on the Father's love for me. I am allowing myself to be on a lifelong journey of growing in Him as He leads. There is no pressure to perform or change myself. Sometimes this feels like nothing is happening, but I remind myself gently to again let go and enjoy what the day brings. It is peaceful inside of me.

"There's just no telling how far I'll go." —Moana

With my heart held wide open, I am beginning to dream again of doing impossible things. I remember a dream I had of being in the midst of a remote jungle tribe. From our trips to Africa, my favorite memories are walking amongst the people and praying for them. I'm not bothered by language barriers because the language of love is common ground. Moreover, when God comes to heal hearts or deliver people from demons, I know I am living in my calling.

FEELING ALIVE

I remember an old woman from South Africa whose eyes beseeched mine with her pain. We had prayed for her son as he worked outside on his car and his leg had been healed. So he invited us inside to pray for his mom. She kept patting her heart, and I knew she was communicating that she had pain in her heart. I began to lead her in letting go, forgiving, and receiving what Jesus had for her, through a partial interpretation from her son. I don't know exactly what Father did, but her happy tears, hugs, and laughter told me it was something good. I feel alive when I am completely dependent on His power like this.

UPSIDE-DOWN KINGDOM

I often think I am living in an upside-down kingdom. Here I had been searching for confidence and freedom in being a certain person that God created me to be, but now I have found freedom has no arrival point. Instead, I trust that both you and I are doing the best we can with the perspective we have at the moment. We are searching for comfort, for belonging, for love. True freedom comes with the acceptance of ourselves. We are free to fail! Weakness is part of the journey. The more I can let go of my so-called abilities, the more I can be one with Christ. There is a flow here, and it is very simple. My arrival point is actually staying in the process and admitting with vulnerability what is happening in my heart—almost delighting in transparency.

I recall my two-year-old daughter and the heart-wrenching expressions on her face as she honestly cried out, "But I don't want to share!" or as she hit the wolf on the page of her story, crying for the little pigs and yelling, "Bad, bad wolf!" Remember the story of my wailing in Cambodia on my son's shoulder? That released a dam inside that I still flow from. What I mean is that when sadness starts filling my heart, it is released in a way that I could never access before, and it feels so good. The emotion is released and changes. This, too, is freedom.

I don't know where Father will lead me, but I am astounded at the joy I am finding in living an ordinary life. Right now, I'm listening to the rain and thunder with my dog curled up beside me. I would love to share the stillness and peace I carry. I am filled with compassion for those who are filled with stress. There is a place of rest, and it is an incredible journey. I would love to help someone. I trust love to compel me, but if I do nothing, I am still valued.

I find beauty in the sliver of the moon on a dark night. I wish often to hear Father's voice in my day, but these days, He is mostly speaking powerfully to me in my dreams at night. I will trust what He is doing. I am thankful that He is my Father, and I only need to hold His hand. It is a wonderful life, and there is a beautiful freedom in being a child.

TWELVE

FREEFALLING IN HIS LOVE

"Those who are loved by God, let his love continually pour from you to one another because God is love. Everyone who loves is fathered by God and experiences an intimate knowledge of him."
—1 John 4:7—

The surprising benefits of doing nothing...

When I think of surrender, I am taken back to my first experience of letting go as a young Christian. My first experience with completely letting go was a complete surprise to me. I'd like to share that story from the beginning of my Christian life and then another recent story with a similar theme.

STORY 1: I'M DONE

After Brett was born, and I believed in God, I told Him straight up what I needed, "Okay, God. What I need is 1. A church, 2. Christian friends, and 3. A Bible study." Having no clue about what sort of church to look for, I start attending a different one each week. I would nervously walk in the front door and ask, "Do you believe in the Bible?... Yes?... Okay."

One Sunday, I found my church home with my list of three things and with great excitement started learning all I could alongside my new friends. Every afternoon, I couldn't wait for my son's nap time so I could devour the Word. In the evening, I went to a Bible study or walked with my friend and talked about God. Every night I'd ask forgiveness for every sin I could think of. My pastor even commented to me one day, "I liked you better before when you didn't know what sin was!" I wasn't quite sure how to take that, so I tried harder. I went to every meeting and every opportunity to learn.

Meanwhile, I was married to a good man, the one I waited for my whole life, and we were working out the issues of living together and coming into agreement. Luckily, in spite of our frequent spats, we loved each other very much, but this was when the battle for control was still on.

One day in the middle of a zesty argument, he shouted point-blank, "Look at you! Two years of being a Christian and you're no different than before! Listen to what just came out of your mouth!"

Shock cascaded over me as the arrow went in. I sputtered in fury, and my lines of defense spewed out accusations, but all my protests and tears were no match for the truth waiting patiently in the air. Stewing helplessly all day and night, knowing that my husband's words were true, I woke early with my decision. I was done. Despite my frantic and passionate efforts, I was no different than before I believed in God. Obviously, this Christian thing was not working.

"I'm done!!" I cried to God in great sorrow mixed with outright anger. "If you want me to live this Christian life, you're going to have to do it YOURSELF!!" I meant it 100%. He could see how hard I had tried—anyone could. I threw in the towel and all my efforts with it and left it all, right in God's hands.

Instantly, I felt a surprising lightness I had never felt before. Everything inside me went quiet. I was floating as I walked around the house. I could only marvel at how wonderful this felt. I recognized that by giving up all my effort, all my striving, and all my ideas of what a Christian should be, including learning everything as fast as I could, was exactly what Father was waiting for.

A peaceful, calm quietness kept me feeling safe and protected. For three days, I lived in the bubble of His Presence and nothing anyone said or did affected me. It felt surreal. In this place of surrender where I wasn't trying to do anything, I felt so happy inside in spite of living in the same tensions of life.

Giving up was the real beginning of my life adventures in the Spirit. I feel like this was the real start of my Christian life as much as I adore the earnest zeal of my young self trying to do what only God can do.

From that time on, the word "surrender" had a whole new meaning for me. It felt in my heart like letting go.

That's it.

Surrender:

- Definition:to give oneself up into the power of another : YIELD
- Synonyms: cede, cough up, deliver, give up, hand over, lay down, relinquish, render, turn in, turn over, yield[1]

I found walking in unity with the Lord one of the trickiest things ever to maintain. It says in the Bible to keep in step with the Spirit. I love this! I am immediately inspired with the words, but the only time that I consistently kept in step with the Spirit was during my season of grieving. This was simply because the pain of being even slightly independent was crushing for me. Truthfully, pain of all sorts has been my best motivator to yield to whatever God was doing in me. Surrendering to God has always been my chief desire, but the problem has been that I simply haven't known what was in my heart. This too is part of what makes Him a good Father. He not only understands my heart but He knows what to do about it. I can completely let go and trust He knows where we're going.

STORY 2: YOU ARE LOVED

We had recently returned home from the 2018 Inheriting the Nations school in New Zealand. As I was living with an open heart, peacefully waiting for Father to show Michael and I our next steps in life, the days and weeks rolled into months.

Life was humming along quietly as we looked after our Airbnb and met with people for prayer on occasion. It was a simple life. I was waiting and waiting to know what we would be doing with our lives. I had a dream that I was in an incubation period of fifteen months. "From when?!" I wondered with much exasperation. Surely not from now! However, I was determined not to run ahead of the Father's plans, so I stayed home enjoying the revelation of being loved by Him and being at home in my heart. Niggling thoughts such as, "I sure hope I'm on the right track!" needed the Father's regular assurance to trust Him. He guided me, mostly through dreams.

One time, I stepped towards a railway track crossing and was almost run over by a long, fast train that came out of nowhere. The Father was teaching me to be patient, a new thing for me. Except for my desire to do something new and meaningful, I simply loved this period of newfound confidence. I thought I was ready for anything but wasn't expecting what came next.

One spring day, I awoke with energy coursing through me. This was highly unusual, and I didn't know if it was good or bad. I told Michael, "We need to climb a mountain today. Let's go on a hike." He complained of a sore back, but nothing would hold me back. I didn't know what it was, but something was rising like a volcano inside of me. Michael looked at me in wonder and agreed to come.

Living near the lake in a mountain town, walking outside means walking uphill. Moving at a good clip, tears immediately started coursing down my cheeks. Michael quietly drew me out with gentle questions and encouragement. I became more and more unsettled until I was bursting with agitation, even anger, still uncertain about what was wrong. All I knew was that I was unhappy. "Unhappy about what?" Michael would ask. I didn't know, I babbled, except that I wasn't doing anything important. Michael pulled gently on that rope until it started unraveling. This is good, he reassured me, just go with it. Something is dying inside you and it needs to fully die so that Father can resurrect it.

As we stomped up through town and entered into the forest path, I began to express all the important things I wanted to do. I wanted to make a difference in the world. I wanted to be on missions. I wanted to walk on water and live in the miracles of God. I wanted to pray for people and see them set free from demons. I could tell something was breaking open inside me. Then all my complaints flowed out about how I was doing nothing—absolutely nothing! Building my table, looking after my Airbnb, even praying for people—it all felt like less than nothing to me, as much as had I enjoyed doing those things. Gradually, I emptied out my heart from the places where subconsciously I had believed my value came from—from doing something of great significance. I wouldn't say I believed this in my head, but my heart told the real story.

WHO AM I THEN?

With the streaming sunlight filtering through the Douglas fir trees, we walked and walked. I tearfully let go of everything I had ever received value from, beginning with achievements and accomplishments. On a roll now, I began moving on to every relationship that gave me any sense of comfort or status, such as being a friend, daughter, sister, or mother. In the end, to my surprise, I even felt to let go of my identity as a child of God. This doesn't make rational sense, but I felt that my status as God's child was somehow propping up my sense of worth, perhaps my status in my own eyes, even though it is a beautiful true identity.

Two emotional hours later, I felt completely vulnerable. I simply prayed, "Father, I've given all of who I am to You. I have let go the best I can." Both of us were deep in the presence of the Holy Spirit. Michael blessed me and prayed for the Father's love to fill me. Clearly, I saw a chalk outline of my body, similar to an image in a crime scene but with shining light all around its circumference. I thought maybe this was a kind of spiritual death.

Although I was feeling completely spent with emotion, I felt light, even exhilarated. I knew something significant had been broken inside me. I felt rather raw, having let go of, in many ways, what mattered to me most. Being part of the local healing rooms team, I went that evening and entered into worship in the hour before the doors opened. The Holy Spirit filled me so completely I wasn't aware of my surroundings, only consumed by His Presence. From deep in my heart I cried out earnestly, "Well, who am I then?"

Without hesitation my heart knew His voice. "You are LOVED," the Father replied softly. His love poured into the emptiness of all that I had surrendered that day. I was held in His powerful love. My identity was deeper than being a child or daughter and especially beyond doing anything. I understood that who I am is rooted in the Source of love: my Father in heaven. It is based on who He is: unchanging love. I can let go of trying to prove myself and discovering who I am or what I am to do. I am worthy of His love.

There is a freedom here that I am beginning to enjoy. I am perfectly happy inside of myself. No doubt, this will be tested, and I hope I can say like Job, "*When he tests me, I will come out as pure gold*" (Job 23:10, NLT). But if I fail, I will hold onto my Father's hand and He will show me how to get back on track. I feel reassured of His love and am so grateful.

From that time, I have not wrestled with what I am doing or will be doing. My significance does not come from accomplishing something or from my relationship with anyone. I am being freed from the weight of being anything to anyone, except to Father. The source of my value has been totally exposed, and my prison doors have been flung wide open. The heart of my insecurity was getting my identity from all my relationships, including thinking I qualified somehow for being a child of God. Ropes were cut every time I let go of a place I had received my value. Chains were unlocked in the spirit realm that I didn't even know were weighing me down. I surrendered the "important work" I thought I should be doing.

What was hidden, perhaps even subconsciously, was brought to light as I gave time and space for things to come up in my heart. If I had been busy, would I have discovered the beautiful identity of "You are loved"? These are the surprising benefits of doing nothing in the kingdom. Again, I am amazed at how the Father is always fathering me. "Doing'" something has been replaced with "being" something.

Who am I?

I am loved.

God's light feels like freedom for me. He has brought light to so many key areas of my heart. Accepting myself has led to accepting other people. Knowing I belong is teaching me to let go of striving to impress anyone. Loving myself is starting to flow into loving people and appreciating their struggle towards peace, belonging, and significance.

The more I let go of the pressure to change myself, the more freedom I give people to live out their journey. Everyone is doing their best to find happiness. The Father is working in all of our hearts. I'm beginning to open my heart to the goodness of who He is. He alone knows the way for me to become increasingly free to receive His goodness, walking out of self-consciousness and being bound up in my personality.

I am discovering a secret to freedom. The secret is in surrendering to the love of God, knowing He is loving me right now. During the day, I often pause and allow my heart to rest in His love. Perhaps there will come a day when this is as natural as breathing, and I look forward to that. These days, I am ecstatic to know that a little reminder that His love is flowing through my heart right now fills me with peace. Here in His love, I can let go of my daily concerns. Sometimes there is frustration or pain that He needs to reveal. In His love, I am not defensive. I am learning that repentance and forgiveness are my shortest path to peace. I imagine Him loving others as well.

I am also trusting the Father is walking with me in my day and bringing meaning to my life. I still want my life to count. My heart is yearning to walk on the water, see angels, and live in the supernatural, but now I recognize that I am living in the supernatural every day. I experience Him in praying for other people. Holding the space with faith and bringing others into an encounter of His love is a good day for me. I trust He will open doors He has planned for me in perfect timing and in spectacular ways. I am finding that these doors can be private or public. For example, it is astounding what He is showing me in my dream life. Once I realized the significance of God speaking to me through dreams, I began seeking the meaning and receiving the insights given. However He is speaking, I am caught in the flow of His transforming love. Freedom is the most beautiful word I know to describe the moment because here I am, learning a new perspective on life.

The Father's love is unwrapping cords of self-consciousness from my heart. Where I was a prisoner to what everyone else thought of me, Abba's love is freeing me to receive value from His view of me. I went from feeling less than to feeling that I was being seen. He is bringing me into His heart where I find safety and belonging. Here I can let go of control a little more. I was found by my Father when I allowed myself to be discovered. Once I invited Him into my lonely and insecure places, He transformed them into jewels called acceptance and confidence. It's a refreshing way to live.

Jesus is bringing all of us together as a family from all around the world. Our differences are what make us beautiful. Uniqueness makes us invaluable. Jesus says that we are all His. He brings us to the Father where we are all His children. We don't need to focus on what we know or don't know here. The Father knows enough for everyone. Rather, we get to be little children, open to His love, and delighting in holding His hand. We are not qualified, and there is no need to consider other people's qualifications. The only thing we need to do is trust in Jesus to qualify us. If He has qualified us, He has qualified everyone else; they just may not know it yet. *Father, help us all to believe and show us what a good Father You are.*

RIVER OF GOD

There is a river of God flowing through our lives. The water is fresh, pure, and clean. The sparkling green color invites us in. Our toes can be seen on the smooth pebbles. The flow of the current is irresistible in fulfilling the desire of our hearts. We walk in deeper. The discoveries are endless and the water is refreshing to our spirits. I see the waterfall from up high, even beyond the universe. I see that I am in one small droplet of water, surrounded in the drop by the Father's love. There are billions of droplets with each one of us inside a droplet. As the droplet falls in the waterfall, I am protected, safe in the Father's love. He is the water. The water is not injured by bumps or scrapes; it flows naturally and easily over the rocks or through the air. There is a place of stillness in the drop of water, even as it freefalls in the waterfall.

Each of the water droplets are like molecules and hold hands with each other. The droplets do not go over the edge alone but are each connected to one another. There is strength in being in connection with each other and also being surrounded by the Father's love and protection. Our hearts long to let go, to spring into the river and be caught in the unstoppable love flowing effortlessly into our being. Here we find life, abundant and overflowing life, full of joy and light-heartedness. Nothing else fills our hearts like being one with the river of life. Laughter bubbles up and sparkling eyes connect with our Creator.

Welcome, child.

In Your light, we see light.

> ***To know you is to experience a flowing fountain, drinking in your life, springing up to satisfy. In your light we receive the light of revelation.***
>
> **—Psalm 36:9**

EPILOGUE

I am doing something brand new,
something unheard of.
Even now it sprouts and grows and matures.
Don't you perceive it?
—Isaiah 43:19—

I'm on the edge of something big. My spirit is stirring, and Papa is unlocking a secret to me. I thought I knew what it meant to be "in Christ." In Christ alone, my hope is found. I depend on Him for everything. He has saved me countless times from despair, fear, anger, hatred, and all kinds of insecurities and doubts—He has saved me from myself.

He has also saved me from others. He has opened doors and closed doors. He has directed my steps in ways beyond my imagination at times. He has taught me keys to the kingdom and blown my mind in how He has brought healing for my heart and used me as a healing vessel for others.

I love Jesus, I love the Father, and I love the Holy Spirit. I love Their Presence, and I often think I cannot live without it. I thought this was the full extent of living "in Christ."

I am holding onto my seat here. I can see everything I knew swirling in gigantic swirls, and again, I'm about to freefall. Everything I knew is being reformed, reconstructed, and maybe, some bits tossed completely. So, I'm teetering on the edge of a precipice, and my knuckles feel white. Do I reach down into the swirling abyss and resurrect the glory of yesterday? Or do I keep in step with the Father into the unknown?

For five years, I've been struggling with whether or not to step back into patterns that brought me to where I am today. Is it okay to let go of what was so good in the hope of something even better? I go back and forth between letting go of the past and surrendering to the new, letting Him lead me through this new transition.

I still pick up my journal and wait for the Spirit to come, but it's not the same! Now I'm simply basking in our communion. I used to love fasting, at least I loved the benefits. I still fast a little, but it feels different now. I recognize that my efforts are not the focus.

If I had to choose, I'd say the Father is doing a new thing. I tell myself, "Trust—let go of the old." If I'm honest, this is a familiar refrain, although each time is no easier. When I am being led into a new season, I have had to let go of the past season and the glory I found there. However, what He has formed in me will be part of me forever, and I take comfort in that.

These days, my dream life is vibrant and new, and I'm learning how to hear Him in "dream parables." He showed me the fence, and I'm to let the past stay in the past. He's showing me that our hearts are where we find true life and beauty. Because I am in Christ, I am fully forgiven when I've done something wrong. While consequences from my poor choices may have to play out, I can confidently come to Him for help, knowing His heart is wide open to me, and He will gently show me the way to go.

Abba, I belong to You! Take me out upon the waters. I need to live in You in a way that depends on You completely.

Which leads me to where I am today: "In Christ." I am starting to see that my Jesus has been limited to what I've known so far and what it means to be in Him has also been way too defined. I want Papa to take me on a grand adventure that blasts me into the reality of the kingdom of heaven. I have some questions. I want to know what it means to be loved by the Trinity and to know each one of them. How can I fully live in the Spirit? ***"To live is Christ,"*** Paul says (Phil. 1:21). What does he mean?

My heart is stirred. The revelation of partaking of the flow of love between Father and Son is lighting my heart on fire. Anticipation is rising. I also feel doubt lurking at the door. No actual words are formed, but I sense a pull towards the familiar way of thinking I've always known. I have loved the way my Christian life has been. Most of all, I love how God has always been there and come through for me in amazing and miraculous ways.

POSSIBILITIES

I am excited. I've been swept up in the love of the Father in depths that have changed me forever. Life keeps getting simpler and simpler. I see my "new land," spacious and free, wild with possibilities. I have hardly even begun to explore my land. I've been busy receiving what He has given me and above all else, letting go, letting go, letting go...

> ***Every spiritual blessing in the heavenly realm has already been lavished upon us as a love gift from our wonderful heavenly Father, the Father of our Lord Jesus—all because he sees us wrapped into Christ. This is why we celebrate him with all our hearts!***
>
> **—Ephesians 1:3**

He even calls me flawless and His perfect one (Song of Songs 4). When I dare to believe these words, I immediately feel like I'm freefalling in His love. It's almost a scary feeling, not knowing how or if I will land. The sensation is one of trust and hope but also awe and a niggling of wonder that He might really be so good! My heart is filled with anticipation, and I love Him so much.

Right now (2020), we are in the midst of COVID-19, tucked away in our homes and only going out for necessities. The whole world has become still, as life as we knew it has come to a halt. We don't know if the future will be anywhere near the same or if this will change life in more ways than we can envision right now. Fear seems to have gripped the planet in many ways, but thankfully, not in my home.

My husband and I are on alert, being careful to wash our hands for 20 seconds at every opportunity and praying no one in our family becomes sick. Zoom calls are our connection with the outside world, with the exception of my pregnant daughter's gender reveal party last evening. We were the only guests, but we cut the pretty cake and celebrated the blue icing inside, indicating we will soon have a grandson. Yay! I'm really excited. Afterward, the streets were eerily silent on the way home, with everyone thankfully tucked inside. The world is crazy quiet.

Right now, my husband is playing "Mercy Street" on his guitar, and I am writing this as we sit by the fireplace in our lofty townhouse. We appreciate the stillness, void of interruptions, so that we can listen to our hearts and do the things we love, as long as it's inside our home. I am partially fasting from sugar and flour, eating healthy while pressing into the Father's heart and tuning in to receive love and revelation from Him. Otherwise, I would be baking cookies, which I also love.

Both of us are excited about the Scriptures and are in the midst of new revelations. Michael is blown away by new depths of understanding in the parables. When I read anything about being "in Christ" these days, my heart explodes in wonder. In spite of the fear outside, undeniable peace fills our hearts. It's like a sanctuary. Peace is our Father, Jesus, and the Holy Spirit. It cannot be forced, but He Himself is peace filling our spirits. He's living in you, too, and I find that comforting. I hope that the Father has revealed His love to you through my little life story.

Many blessings and much love,

Chara

NOTES

1. Found

1. Lyrics from *Out of Hiding* written by Stephanie Gretzinger & Amanda Cook

2. Unravelling

1. Simmons, Brian. The Passion Translation The New Testament with Psalms, Proverbs, and Song of Songs, Second Edition BroadStreet Publishing Group, LLC, 2018, page 279.

3. Wilderness

1. King, Helene, speaker at Fatherheart Ministries Inheriting the Nations school, Orama, New Zealand, September 2018
2. Moore, Beth. Believing God, Experiencing a Fresh Explosion of Faith, Member Book, Lifeway Press, Nashville, 2003, 73-93

4. Faith

1. July 9, 2020, Oh My Disney, Peter Pan Quotes: The Ultimate List of Peter Pan Quotes https://ohmy.disney.com/quotes/2018/03/26/ultimate-list-peter-pan-quotes/

5. Heart Healing

1. Dass Supperamanium, Speaker & Director of Inheriting the Nations School, Orama, New Zealand, October, 2018

7. Tragedy

1. Rick Joyner, "The Final Quest", Fort Mill, SC, Morningstar Publications, Inc, 2010, loc 741 of 1912 Kindle Edition

9. Love Falls Down

1. Jordan, M. James. The Ancient Road Rediscovered: What the Early Church knew... (p. 94). Fatherheart Ministries. Kindle Edition.
2. Jordan, M. James. The Ancient Road Rediscovered: What the Early Church knew... (p. 35). Fatherheart Ministries. Kindle Edition.
3. Jordan, M. James. The Ancient Road Rediscovered: What the Early Church knew... (p. 40). Fatherheart Ministries. Kindle Edition.
4. Jordan, M. James. The Ancient Road Rediscovered: What the Early Church knew... (p. 50). Fatherheart Ministries. Kindle Edition.
5. Jordan, M. James. The Ancient Road Rediscovered: What the Early Church knew... (p. 68). Fatherheart Ministries. Kindle Edition.

10. Home

1. Helene King. Orama, Great Barrier Island, New Zealand, a speaker at Inheriting the Nations School, Oct. 3, 2018
2. Jordan, M. James. The Ancient Road Rediscovered: What the Early Church knew... (p. 12). Fatherheart Ministries. Kindle Edition.
3. Jordan, M. James. The Ancient Road Rediscovered: What the Early Church knew... (pp. 15-16). Fatherheart Ministries. Kindle Edition.

11. Free to be Me

1. Bush, Lousie; Cravalho, Aulii; House, Rachel; Jackson, Christopher; Scherzinger, Nicole. "Where You Are." *Moana* (2016).

12. Freefalling in His Love

1. Merriam-Webster's Collegiate Dictionary (10th ed.). (1999). Merriam-Webster Incorporated.

ABOUT THE AUTHOR

Chara is a passionate seeker of life and is often described as encourager and motivator to those around her by life example. She loves to live spontaneously and has traveled extensively around the world, with a heart for Europe, Africa, and the Middle East. Intimacy with God and open-hearted relationships with people are what gives her life. She is not intimidated by life's challenges and is known to partner with God's heart to achieve the miraculous.

Her accomplishments have been raising 2 amazing children, organizing and opening a class 1 private Christian school of which she was principal and teacher, and vital participation in a healing prayer ministry. Her love for healing prayer stems from the freedom Father brought to her own heart to bring her from being self-conscious and insecure to confident in living as a beloved daughter of God.

Chara has discovered joy by following her heart. Above all, she loves to pray and connect with others and help them to find confidence and freedom to live in the midst of love and acceptance. You might also find her sanding wood for her next wood project or cooking creatively for her husband and friends. Hers is a journey of finding freedom through experiencing Father's love where we all can find belonging in the family of God.